"Reading this book feels like having a wise and keenly observant uncle tell you everything they've learned about how to not be miserable. If you're ready to stop being an asshole to yourself and need more than fluffy affirmations, this book is for you." **—NADIA BOLZ-WEBER**, podcast host of *The Confessional*, author of *Shameless*

"A playful and compassionate book about confronting the mental chatter that keeps us from mental peace and quiet. Neal Allen writes as a friend and guide ready to put an arm around you and say, 'Let's see if we can get the neighbors to pipe down a bit.'" **—KATE BOWLER,** author of *No Cure for Being Human (And Other Truths I Need to Hear)* and *Everything Happens for a Reason (And Other Lies I've Loved)*

"With penetrating clarity and lightheartedness, the author walks us through a remarkably accessible and effective method for dismantling the critical voice that has convinced almost all of us that we are separate and doomed. The spaciousness and ease that flow into the space that bossy little 'gremlin' used to take up transform daily life from an anxious trudge into a tender adventure. Highly recommended." **—MIRABAI STARR,** author of *Caravan of No Despair* and *Wild Mercy*

"In Neal Allen's book, you'll find a tool to help meet one of the most daunting challenges to a better life: that voice that has taken up residence inside you and berates, cajoles, warns you every step of the way. The tool can help you sleep better, work better, help you find a sense of ease in your life." **—JEFF GREENFIELD,** author, veteran TV network political analyst

"In Better Days, the mean, soul-crushing voice we all endure is addressed by Neal Allen with grace and wisdom born of direct experience. His kind voice models all that he is teaching so that as we read, we are steeped in kindness itself. Beautiful." **—GENEEN ROTH,** bestselling author of *Women Food and God*

BETTER DAYS

TAME YOUR INNER CRITIC

NEAL ALLEN

BETTER DAYS

TAME YOUR INNER CRITIC

NEAL ALLEN

books that change your life

namaste

PUBLISHING

VANCOUVER, CANADA

ISBN 978-1-897238-84-4 (Hardcover) | ISBN 978-1-897238-85-1 (Softcover)

Library and Archives Canada Cataloguing in Publication

Title: Better days : tame your inner critic / Neal Allen; with foreword by Anne Lamott.
Names: Allen, Neal (spiritual coach), author.
Identifiers: Canadiana 20230185886 | ISBN 9781897238844 (hardcover) | ISBN 9781897238851 (softcover)

Subjects: LCSH: Self-confidence. | LCSH: Self-talk. | LCSH: Self-acceptance. | LCSH: Criticism, Personal.

Classification: LCC BF575.S39 A45 2023 | DDC 158.1—dc23

This book is meant to be informative, not prescriptive. The author of this book does not dispense medical advice or prescribe the use of any technique or practice as a form of treatment for physical, mental, emotional, or medical problems without the advice of a qualified physician, either directly or indirectly. The intent of the author is only to offer information of a general nature to help you in your quest for emotional and spiritual well-being. In the event that you use any of the information in this book for yourself or another, the author and the publisher assume no responsibility for your actions and their consequences.

Selection from R.D. Laing's Knots, 1st Edition by Vintage Books, published by Routledge, © 1970 by The R.D. Laing Trust, reproduced by arrangement with Taylor & Francis Group.

Published by:

Namaste Publishing Inc.
Vancouver BC, Canada

Distributed in North America by Ingram/Publishers Group West

Cover and Interior Book Design: Zoe Norvell
Cover and Interior Illustrations: Amyisla Mccombie

Printed in Canada by Friesens

ALSO BY NAMASTE PUBLISHING

The Power of Now, Eckhart Tolle

A New Earth, Eckhart Tolle

Stillness Speaks, Eckhart Tolle

The Conscious Parent, Dr. Shefali Tsabary

Out of Control, Dr. Shefali Tsabary

The HOW to Inner Peace, Constance Kellough

The Presence Process, Michael Brown

Alchemy of the Heart, Michael Brown

The Revolutionary Trauma Release Process, Dr. David Berceli

for Annie

TABLE OF CONTENTS

FOREWORD

Neal Allen brought up his work with taming the inner critic on our third date, seven years ago. Because I loved his mind, his humor and his nose so much and had already decided I could spend the rest of my life talking with him about spirit, soul, consciousness, JonBenét Ramsey, and movies, I indulged him. The inner critic is a subject I had written about extensively (sometimes as KFKD radio) and had discussed in therapy for decades - that belittling voice inside me that kept me feeling small and afraid. What could he add to my vast and erudite knowledge? Still, I didn't interrupt much. I couldn't resist him: He also had beautiful hands.

I admit that there was this one tiny way in which my understanding might have been a bit incomplete: Never once in all my studies of it had the snarky voice gone away or even grown quieter. So there was that. It liked to hang out with me everywhere I went, keeping a running commentary on all the dangers lurking everywhere, even at church, and how disappointing it found me. It was so omnipresent that I hardly noticed it as

a phenomenon, what Neal described to me that day as a parasite. I didn't
consider it a separate being trying to keep precious little me under its
control, over and over throughout my tasks. Like most people, I thought it
was part of me. It-me had opinions on my writing, on how my butt looked
in my new pants, on how I fold fitted sheets. It said, "Don't do that, you'll
mess it up," or "Do that better or everyone will see that you are a fraud," or
"Don't do anything, you don't know what you are doing." Luckily for me, it
had all the answers. It drowned out Siri, who so nicely told me how many
more yards to the next right turn, issuing red alerts about possible open
manholes, or carjackers, or an impending stroke. It reminded me over and
over how it had helped keep me alive when I was young by having me
freeze on the curb and not run into the street, or stay in the shallow water,
or get males to value me by not shining too brightly or get females to value
me by being a perfect big girl helper.

But that was sixty years ago. I was now very good at traffic and water
safety, and while I hate to brag, at folding fitted sheets. Most of the time,
I became conscious of my inner critic (eventually) when I was sucking up
to people to ensure my worth and inclusion. Well, maybe "most" is too
strong a word. Let's say "sometimes," or "every so often."

So here was Neal with his brilliant mind and cute nose sharing his
insights about how we can learn to quiet this sometimes shaming, sometimes seductive voice that tells me I need to improve or not try anything
new at which I might fail, and in fact almost certainly will. I was listening,
just as on my first date I had been sucked in by his interior body work that
became his somewhat more woo-woo, shall we say, book *Shapes of Truth*.
Dating spiritual types can be trippy.

Under Neal's tutelage, I finally made direct contact with my own inner
critic. I had thought it was me all along, damaged old neurotic me, endlessly self-effacing at best, brutal at worst, sending me down the shame
spiral when a colleague or friend or relative expressed anything less than
adoration and respect. But Neal taught me about its parasitic nature,
a frowning voice from early childhood injected by the culture to socialize

me, learn the rules, and remind me that I am a worm in a sea of hungry fish. No matter who was hosting the parasite – me, you, Neal, Bill Clinton – it told them the same things: that they were doomed without its strict rules, and constantly in danger of being hurt, or walked all over. It told me I couldn't trust anyone, except it, of course. It told me that I'm not good enough, that I'm a fake, that I need to work my butt off in order to be loved. And from the day of its entry into my life when I was six or seven, it never stopped telling me this. Not when I was ten or twenty or fifty. Or even now, in my dotage. It warns me of danger afoot just before I go onstage, or when I open the doors to my family for big holiday dinners. At Whole Foods it makes sure the other people in line, plus the checker, all find me wonderful. It tells me to use my life force to get other people to feel indebted by my acts of generosity and martyrdom: If enough people feel beholden to me because I've done so much to get them to love and need me, I am of value. At least briefly. It's a kind of toxic currency. It tells me to stay home or in my lane or in a safe harbor, and always, always to stay small and alert.

Its messages are the exact opposite of everything I have worked toward for decades, the awakening to presence and loving awareness, my sacred birthright to living a big, juicy life.

With Neal's coaching, I didn't just meet the bad actor who accompanies me. I have learned to identify its voice when it sets about its unholy work, have learned to say to it, nicely, "Oh, that's just you again," and then to get on with my earthly and spiritual work of becoming, of discarding all the false identities it taught me to present to the world, of breathing more expansively, of loving less afraid.

Our friend Duncan Trussell says that when you first encounter him, you're meeting his bodyguard. *Better Days* is about freeing the bodyguard – the creature who molds your shiny, socially acceptable outer shell – to find other work besides monitoring, scaring, and belittling your true, wild, vulnerable, lovingkindness self. Maybe you can find it a job protecting your junk piled in the storage shed, but unless you are still six or seven you otherwise probably do not need its anxious input. You can make pretty good decisions all by yourself without the shopworn advice of a hectoring nag. Maybe you can store your inner critic in the trunk of your car where it can make sure no one steals your beach blanket, poncho, and the emergency hand crank radio you got for subscribing to NPR. But you? As in the you who are built on kindness, not distrust? You are free to ignore its withering gaze and voice, to tune it out like you do your cranky Uncle Ed at holiday meals, and tune in instead to what is true and maybe even lovely, like sweet cousin Jill and her famous cherry pie.

You are free to go take a walk despite the voice insisting you should read over your proposal one more time. You are free to wander and ponder the beauty of this earth, your neighbors, the clouds, instead of the numbers on your bathroom scale, your checking account, or the latest polls. You are free to notice that you can live your life from a place of satisfaction and gratitude, rather than anxiety and bean-counting and constriction. You are free to love the world as it is, free from obsessing about what is so wrong with everything and how you probably caused it but, in any case, definitely need to fix it; free to live this one precious life from a place of awareness and trust. You are free to be your own kind of saint, meeting people with love and curiosity rather than pity or fear.

Better Days will help you get to know your inner critic and quiet its yammering, and in so doing get to know the person you were born to be. Rather than believing what the ego tells you – that your great advantage is your unique and superior self, an idea that has kept you separate from life, yourself, others, and God – you will meet the being of kindness, intimacy, commonality. No other system has ever so efficiently broken through my lifelong sense of isolation as the work you are about to encounter, and at the same time been so welcoming and even fun. And while I can hear my own critic whisper that I should do one or two more drafts of this introduction, I am instead saying to it gently, "Oh, that's just you again," while I expertly tie my shoes and bounce on out into the light of a new morning.

—Anne Lamott

Fairfax, California

"According to the Buddhist tradition, the spiritual path is the process of cutting through our confusion, of uncovering the awakened state of mind. When the awakened state of mind is crowded in by ego and its attendant paranoia, it takes on the character of an underlying instinct. So it is not a matter of building up the awakened state of mind, but rather of burning out the confusions which obstruct it."

—Chögyam Trungpa, *Cutting Through Spiritual Materialism*

ONE

HELLO, PARASITE

A parasite whispers to me, delivering a running commentary and haranguing me with nonstop advice. Attached to my cranium, it bypasses my ears and drills straight into my mind. It's mostly a nag and fearmonger, but now and again this bloodsucker calls me names. "Fraud." "Idiot." "Loser." I seldom notice it, so I don't really think it's there. But left to its own devices, the messages will cut through all the time, damaging my psyche day after day.

My wife calls hers The Governess. Mine's The Gremlin. You have one, too. Everybody does. It's your inner critic.

If you wake up confident and raring to go, by noon it has beaten your self-esteem to a pulp. It warns you of all your potential screw-ups – next week's and the one coming in ten seconds. It makes you feel miserable, or less-than, or unwanted, or doomed. It's your own personal, relentless, constant buzzkill.

If you've been a little frustrated in your on-again, off-again quest for satisfaction, ease, or consistent love, follow me. The path to personal nirvana is routed through your inner critic. It isn't you; it's your own personal parasite that torments you with bad thoughts, pressures you to perform perfectly or not at all, sneers at your mistakes, separates you from your family, and keeps you relentlessly uncertain about yourself.

Freud discovered this parasite more than 100 years ago*. Its scientific name in English is "superego." You've got one attached to you, I've got one, we've all got one. Freud believed that it was necessary in human development, and that its purpose was to override our impulses and keep us in line, socially and ethically. Another name for it is "conscience," which sounds good and helpful. It's a miniature storehouse of the social rules and conventions, personalized for you. Freud wouldn't have called it a parasite: He believed that it was fully embedded in a three-part human personality, nestled in as a part of the core self. He said the superego is you just as much as your survival and libido impulses – your instincts – are you.

I beg to differ. I've gotten to know my parasitic superego. It's a construction, a facsimile of a person, with its own distinct personality. It doesn't sit inside me. It hovers just outside, a whisperer. It's a humanoid creature. I have conversations with it. It's about as embedded and present as a four-year-old's imaginary friend.

The parasite and its foul mouth are the bad news. The good news is that I have quieted mine, and you can immobilize yours, too. It's pretty simple. If you long for a life of freedom, of peace of mind and satisfaction, I can show you how.

*Freud's two masterpiece works on the id, superego, and their relationship to civilized life are 1923's *The Ego and the Id* (1960 English translation by James Strachey) and 1929's *Civilization and its Discontents* (1961 Strachey). His brief in *The Ego and the Id* on anxiety and its absolute reliance on the parental frown is startlingly fresh.

TWO

FIRST GRADE: PARADISE LOST

J ade was dragging as she trudged home one Friday in early September. After three days of first grade, her head was spinning. Where were the learning-and-play stations of her kindergarten? Why no mat in the middle of the floor? What was this business of sitting in a chair for forty-five minutes without moving?

For the first five years of life, Jade had been immersed in a relatively seamless kid-world. One moment she was lying in the grass, the next playing house with her brother, the next making animal noises, the next running in for a snack, and on and on. Things appeared, started, ended, appeared, started, ended, over and over without rhyme or reason. There weren't a lot of rules. "No" was a word that appeared in the little girl's life more episodically than in a recognizable pattern, even if her parents thought otherwise. Ethics were unknown. A lack of concern about values or right and wrong worked because Jade, like most kids, was rigged to the good, and parents are by and large protective. When Jade was told she had done something bad, her first reaction typically was surprise: "What did I do?"

Even as parents with our own children, we might not notice how innocent children are, and how lacking in pattern recognition and memory. But tell the truth. How many memories do you have before five years old? A few, sure, but memory is not a well-developed faculty yet. It doesn't need to be, so long as adults are constantly hovering, ready to scoop you out of harm's way. Are you sure you were a fully conscious, thoughtful being in those early years? Maybe you just went along with the world as it showed up to you. What need did you have for remembering what happened yesterday?

Memories are stored for pattern recognition, so a danger can be averted or a wish can be fulfilled. We think memories just happen, and store themselves, but it isn't like that. They're curated. And they're not particularly accurate. They're little fairy tales, each one of them. We store only that part of the experience that offers a useful cause-and-effect pattern. All the complexity is removed. What's left is something like this: When I was six and hit my little brother, I got sent to my room. When I smiled sweetly, I got a second scoop on my cone. Most of what's unrelated to the moral is forgotten. I can't even remember the taste of the second scoop, or who scooped it for me, just that I won it.

For all of us, as for Jade, memories start to multiply and things change at around six or seven. Whether Jade is raised in India or Senegal or America, it happens the same way. The outside culture decides it's time for Jade to grow up. Over the first few days of first grade, her whole world is turned topsy-turvy. No more self-directed play. No more cruising from station to station in the preschool or kindergarten classroom. No more tugging on the teacher's sleeve for help. Instead, it's time to learn to read – for everyone in the class at the same time, for forty-five minutes. Sit still for those forty-five minutes. Raise your hand if you have a question and wait until you're called on.

This is some weird stuff to the little kid first confronting it. No one is explaining the usefulness of the structure for maturation or apologizing for the abrupt end to the child's freedom. No one says, "Kid, it's time to grow up."

But after a few days or weeks, after being corrected for getting out of her seat before the forty-five minutes were up, or not raising her hand, or working on arithmetic during reading time, Jade figures it out. "My job is to grow up and become one of those giant adults who lead those peculiar lives above me, and in the meantime get them to approve of me."

Jade might look around for a picture book with instructions, but there isn't one. Her older brother is no help. He was never told that this is all about socializing and growing up to be a productive adult either. He just shrugs and tells her to go along with it and stay out of trouble.

Everywhere Jade looks, there's a new expectation for her to obey a new rule. Everything has become deadly serious all of a sudden. Regimented and serious. Her life isn't sad or happy so much as it is perplexing.

Jade is confused. Everybody is in the same boat in the first days of first grade. Everybody is confused.

As it slowly dawns on Jade that her job now is to grow up and become a giant adult, she is greatly troubled. How is that possible? She's just a kid. She doesn't know anything much. She has no idea how the adults implement and carry out all these rules. They're not just hard to figure out, most of them seem invisible. In the most basic ways, she has no idea how the world works. She knows Mommy goes to work every day, but what is "work?" Where does she go? What does she do there? Is it like school? Is it the same as this thing they're now talking about called "schoolwork?" When I was a child, I'm told, my belief was that my dad's "work" was conducted on the bus I saw him step into at the end of our street. All those dads working away on those buses! Nobody told me otherwise. How was I to know better?

The stakes are confusing, too. Jade knows she is supposed to mature into an adult, but she isn't told how, or when, or what will happen if she fails. She is never told that it's one step at a time, and that she doesn't have to figure it out overnight. She isn't told that just about everyone succeeds, and that it's not that big of a deal. All the big adults seem in on the game, and the expectations, but they seem to ignore that she's just a kid. She knows that her mother and father, or someone else big and important, have taken care of her up to now. They've invisibly filled in all the blanks. But now *all* the adults, even strangers, are demanding that she understand the new rules. Jade is overwhelmed, and she doesn't always have Mom or Dad to help her out.

One day early in first grade, just as Jade is resigned to failing her parents and being pawned off on a neighbor, a little voice shows up in her head, saying, "I've got this, kid."

If her newly emerging superego were inclined to explain itself, it might say this to Jade: "I'm going to help you out with the new rules, when your parents aren't around. Here's what we'll do. You know how your mom is more patient with you when you're acting quiet and what she calls 'lady-like'? Well, I'm going to remind you of that every time you're in a confusing situation with an adult woman. You know how your dad gets into a good mood when you joke around with him? Well, I'm going to remind you of that every time you're in a confusing situation with an adult man. And we'll see what happens. I think you'll be pleased."

Jade now has two strategies, one for women like her first-grade teacher and mom's friends, and one for men like her dad and grandpa and the male crossing guard on the way to school.

The strategies of the superego voice – "act ladylike" and "make him laugh" – aren't specific to any of the new rules. They are generic behaviors. But each time she remembers one, it buys Jade time. While she's projecting ladylike poise or goofy charm, she can figure out her next step based on the cues adults offer, as they nod approvingly and pay friendly attention to her. She has to learn the basic social restraints, and the superego is helping her along.

At first, that was all there was to it. The little voice in Jade's head gave her a way to move around adults when her parents weren't around, and it was enough. The rules piled on, and she slowly learned them and stored them away for future use.

If that's all the superego had delivered, Jade would forever cherish it for having saved her life when she was a little kid. Unfortunately for Jade, and for all of us when we were her age, the superego had just gotten started.

THREE

MEET YOUR INNER CRITIC

L isten to the voice in your head, the one that nags you when you're behind in your work. Call it up now and pay attention as it talks to you. What are its inflections? Have you heard those inflections before? Do they remind you of anyone?

In my experience with my clients, the great majority notice that their superego voice sounds like their mother when she was cross. Some find that it sounds more like Dad. A few cannot differentiate it from their own voice, and a tiny few don't hear the voice at all. But it's still there, and so long as you experience everyday conflicts with others, your superego is active behind the scenes.

Psychologists call the process that delivers a superego into our life "introjection," which is one of the coolest words ever. It means the unconscious adoption of another person's beliefs. "Introjection" sounds like science fiction, like I've been stuck with a needle in my neck, and a syringe containing Mom or Dad or another primary caretaker's disappointed voice has emptied into my carotid arteries. And that perfectly describes what has happened. Now that Jade's superego has taken root, it's starting to take over. She has her mom's voice and beliefs inside her, correcting her wherever she goes. Jade hears the voice in her bedroom, in the yard, at school, with her friends, and, eventually, even at the dinner table with mom sitting a few feet away.

Any chance it gets, any opening of spare time, and the superego starts in on Jade.

But its talent was to give Jade a way to interact with adults in confusing situations. What's it doing here, now, even when adults aren't around?

Somehow, the superego decided to be *uber*mom or *uber*dad. Instead of just helping out here and there, it took over. It figured out how to control Jade and liked the work. It kept its job long after she had figured out other ways to buy time and get what she wanted in the confusing world of adults.

Jade's superego broadened itself to become Internalized Mom, and by "Mom," I mean "Mom or Dad or teacher or boss or cop or any old authority figure you name." All those rules of maturity that threw Jade for a loop? It turns out that all the rules are in service of something called socialization, and her superego decided that it was the expert.

Here's where things turn ugly. I hate this part. The story becomes overwrought, dismal, and dooms Jade and everyone like her – which is to say, you and me – to a life rife with insecurity. The superego takes charge of everything, and in its soft, mean whisper it criticizes us dozens of times a day, relentlessly. If I glance in the mirror I see my crooked parts. If I miss the trash basket, I get jeered as a kid failing on the schoolyard. If my joke is met with silence, I bow in shame. If I forget a word, I'm heading to senility. If my spouse forgets to say hello, I'm unloved and, quite possibly, unlovable. Life becomes a minefield, and I never notice that there aren't any real mines. It feels like I'm failing, but I'm well-fed, well-clothed, and well-housed for the most part.

As civilized people, *most* of us don't actually worry about our own survival on a typical day. In droughts, we have grocery stores. Our homes are made of stone or wood. We have systems of justice, faulty or not, to keep violence down. Of course, an enormous number of people are deprived: About a half billion people will go to bed hungry tonight. As socially concerned adults, we pay attention to fixing that. But it is also true that 7.5 billion people will go to bed with full bellies tonight, a higher percentage than ever before.

What we get in return for not worrying about basic survival is ceaseless anxiety over non-survival concerns. People in Stone-Age societies* (some still exist on Earth) spend all day talking about falling out of trees, the last drought, and the enemy tribe nearby. They don't live next door to strangers, so they default to trust. Hoarding is hard to do without being caught, so envy isn't prominent. What's there left to think about? Lions, floods, pestilence – the sorts of things that modern man has more or less conquered. Stone-Agers have a large concern about the *id*, or instinctual, side of life – survival – and little concern with the superego side of life – civilization.

As modern, civilized people, we fill our days with non-survival concerns, almost all of which orbit around productivity. Our superego allows a ranked, hierarchical system to feed and house gazillions of people who lack much tribal sameness. Civilization is based on mistrust. All our rules, from looking both ways before crossing the street to not trespassing on private property to being expected to work forty hours a week at a dull job, are for the benefit of the civilization prospering. What is meant by prospering? That's simple. It's mostly biological. Our rules are designed to keep the species spreading and growing, filling niches in the Darwinian closed system. We're probably second-best at the task, runners-up to bacteria. Which isn't to say that we're strictly biological animals. Quite the opposite. We have souls. We have choice. We have

---

*Most of my references to Stone-Age societies, based on existing tribes, were learned from Jared Diamond's *The World Until Yesterday: What Can We Learn from Traditional Societies?* (New York: Penguin 2012), Yval Noah Haran's *Sapiens: A Brief History of Humankind* (New York: Harper 2015), and Joe Kane's *Savages* (New York: Knopf 1997). My interest was first piqued by meeting some members of the tribe that Kane wrote about on a two-day visit in the Ecuadorian jungle.

the potential for freedom. Civilization certainly has its benefits, but along with these, imposes the view that we're strictly biological animals by depriving us of our humanity – our ability to trust and share – and replacing it with productivity, rules, and ethics, which require hierarchies to keep everybody working on the difficult task of the common good – species survival. Civilization gives us justice systems, bosses, wage slavery and general distrust. Ask any anthropologist.

And the manager of justice systems, bosses, wage slavery, and distrust is our social ruleset – overlapping political, familial, and religious ethical systems and arbitrary regulations that are supposed to guide our every movement. As adults, you would think that we could read the rules and adopt them and that would be that. Our superego doesn't let us do that. It says we are not adults, and that its abridged set of the social rules must be hauled out and recited to us hour after hour, day after day. It says that we can't be trusted with knowing the rules but must stay under the whip of the superego's own bullying, punishing, enslaving voice. When we complain, it shrugs and adds sarcastically, "You think you're different from everybody else?"

We can't go back to being cavepeople, and there's no sense trying to replace civilized rules with tribal patterns. Eating organically isn't going to magically erase the need for a global transportation infrastructure that moves massive amounts of food into communities that lack the soil, sun, or water to feed themselves. Communal living experiments break down into the same petty squabbling that leads their suburban counterparts to erect fences.

So, we're stuck with the drudgery of mistrust and productivity? We're stuck in the land of the superego? We have a pretend mom or dad or school principal waving its finger at us for our share of eternity?

Wrong.

FOUR

CONFRONT YOUR INNER CRITIC

We have a way out. It's staring us in the face, but it's not obvious. That's because the nagging, insistent voice of the superego hides. It expends most of its effort as a scarcely discernible whisper. Psychologists say it resides in my subconscious mind, but they're wrong. It's not subconscious: My superego attaches to the outside of my mind, not to a layer deep within me. It's not subconscious; it's subvocal. It hides by not talking very loudly. If I wanted to hear it vocally I could. I just don't bother most of the time, and it takes advantage of that.

My superego is a vampire. If I allow it to stay in the dark, in a subvocal nagging, in a quiet drone of continual narration, it gets its way. It influences me in near silence. If I bring it up to my hearing – to the light of day, so to speak – it loses its life force and can even disintegrate. It doesn't like to be heard directly, loudly. And for a good reason. It's an idiot who has no business running my life. It's deathly afraid I'll find that out, and so it stays subvocal as much as possible.

My only job, it turns out, is to bring the voice of my superego to the surface. I just need to hear it.

Which isn't hard to do. It's a little weird, though. I'll take you through the steps.

First, stay seated and locate the voice in your head. Listen for it. When you're mad at yourself, where does the debate rage? For most of the hundreds of people I've coached in private practice and workshops, the voice is located behind the ears, just outside or inside the back of the head. It can't burrow very deep. Your true self gets in the way. Some people hear it more in the top of the cranium or even in the forehead. A few find it elsewhere in or around the body.

Mentally, find where in or near your body the voice is located, then stretch one arm stiffly in front of you, palm up and facing you. Pull the voice from the back of your head, or wherever you hear it, and place it in the palm you are looking at. If you can't find the voice, just pretend you have and hold your hand out.

Wait there and let the voice assume a shape in your palm. This can take a few seconds, or a minute. It might form into a person or a creature or an inanimate object. It might be small or large. The form it takes during this exercise will be its default form forever. It can change and morph, but it will return to the person or creature or object that first appears to you. It will probably look a little cartoonish, but it will also have a sense of reality that differs from your everyday imagination.

Usually, the face is oddly vague, as if slightly blurred. It may seem to have a blank or snide expression. Some have a gender, some don't. It doesn't matter. If a face doesn't show up, pretend that it has, and go on to the next step.

Now that it's propped in front of you, you're ready to start a dialogue with your superego. Yes, you can talk to your superego, even if it's not quite visible. And even cooler, it will answer you back.

What do you want to know from it? I've found a few standard questions are useful to get things started. When you ask it a question, wait patiently for it to answer. It may respond with a facial expression instead of words. Ask the question again, until it responds verbally. Your superego does not like being pinned down, so it will avoid questions if possible. But it will eventually answer if you persist.

Here are my first three standard questions:

"Who put you in charge?"

"When did you take charge?"

"Why are you still in charge?"

Almost all superegos respond to these three questions the same way. I won't spoil your experience by telling you the typical responses here. I want to give you the chance to have a full, unbiased encounter with your superego before considering the results of your first interview. In the next chapter, I'll discuss the universality of superego beliefs. In the meantime, if you haven't already, go ahead and start your dialogue with your own superego.

Once you have satisfactorily heard your superego's answers to the first three questions, continue the questioning.

"I would like to take charge for a while. Will you let me?"

"What are you worried might happen to me if I take charge?"

"What are you worried might happen to you if I take charge?"

Without giving up too much, I'll say that at this point, the superego has become somewhat uneasy about its own future. Continuing the dialogue:

"I promise I will not annihilate you. I need you to let me take charge. We'll do it as an experiment. You'll let me take charge for a while. You'll step aside. We'll see how it goes. Is that OK?"

"I need an affirmative answer, yes or no. Is that OK?"

Once your superego has agreed to the experiment, verbally, it's time to end the dialogue. I find it helpful to end on an optimistic note.

"I'll bet it has been tiring to be in charge for all these years. Has it?"

"Wouldn't it be nice to be retired?"

"I am not getting rid of you. I'm asking you to go into semi-retirement. You can come out and help me when I ask, or when things get too much for me. Your new job title will be Occasional Ethical Adviser. Is that OK with you?"

"Before we go, I want to thank you for saving my life when I was a kid.

I couldn't have made it through those hard times without you."

After closing, restore your superego to its usual place, at the back of your head or elsewhere.

FIVE

TAKE CHARGE

What just happened? Who were you talking to? What kind of craziness is this?

You just met your superego. You found out that it is outside of you, and talks. You found out that it has the facsimile of a life, but a life both different from yours and separate from you. Depending on how it appeared, it is a creature, person, or thing. The form doesn't matter. Because its one job is verbal communication with you, its voice and facial cues are available for discussion, and the rest blurs away.

Your first question was "Who put you in charge?" It's a good bet that your superego answered, "You did." About 90 percent of my clients hear that answer. The remaining 10 percent is divided between "Your mother did," "Your father did," "Your grandmother did," or someone else did. A few superegos are clever enough to say, "I did," but on further probing they agree that they received outside authorization.

In a way, it's true that you put your superego in charge. In its early years, you took full advantage of it. It helped you grow up. I'll show you in

31

what ways later. The good thing to know is that since you were the one who authorized it, you also have the power and right to de-authorize it. We'll get to that.

Your second question was "When did you take charge?" The two most common answers the superego gives are: "I've always been in charge" and "When you were [pick an age between four and ten] years old." A few say, "I don't know," and a tiny number date themselves to the host's adolescence.

In fact, almost all superegos take charge around six, seven, or eight years old. While you learned a little before those years – some counting, maybe even reading – most of your intellectual maturation, at least from the standard of being useful to society, begins at around seven. As Jade learned, first grade is a quantum leap from kindergarten. It's a time for rapid absorption of new ideas, sudden responsibilities, and confusing instructions. But conversely, it's also the time when your parents or teachers stop hovering and checking in on you every fifteen minutes. You are making decisions, some that could be fateful, outside their presence. In a way, you have freed yourself from their harnesses, but it's scary and daunting.

Here's another exercise before we go on. Listen to your superego's whispery voice in or around you in its usual invisibility back behind your ears. Do its inflections, the changes in pitch and tone, remind you of anybody? Anybody? Anybody? The majority of superegos have the inflections of the host's mother. A lot of the remainder have the inflections of the father. The final fraction is divided among another early caregiver, yourself, or an unknown person.

The superego commonly takes on a parent's voice because that's what the superego is: a substitute parent. Jade is at school, being asked to sit in rows and pay attention to a lecturer up front, and she's not sure how to do what she's been told. She wants to get the new rules right, but her mom or dad or grandma isn't around to correct her. The superego pops up and says, "I'll correct you. I'll keep tabs of the rules and remind you of them. I'm here to help." It's a good idea, but it has one fatal deficiency. The superego at this point doesn't actually know the rules very well. It's as new to the game as Jade is. Over time, it will gather events into memory and provide her with pattern recognition. But at first, it doesn't have a memory base to work with. It just has her mother or father's scolding tone.

Scolding or belittling or correcting all carry with them the punishment of distaste. You are distasteful or possibly disgusting if you are prone to getting things wrong. Implied is that there's something wrong with you, or you're unlovable, or at least undesirable. Jade doesn't need a belt or fist to be cowed. A frown is punishment enough. The inflections of the superego are punishment. Just as a scolding parent motivates corrective behavior, so can a snarky superego's inflections.

The superego teaches by threatening punishment, and when you get it wrong, going through with the punishment. When you fail to follow a rule appropriately, the voice whispers, "You idiot. You did it again. How could you be so dumb?" We carry our frowning parent or caregiver with us, in a little voice muttering into our brains. Most of us have the same magnitude superego whispering little warnings. Those few of us who were physically tortured as children or who are afflicted with schizophrenia have outsized superegos that require different solutions than are found in this book. For the great sweep of humanity, our superegos are stunningly similar in size and attitude.

One more exercise helps you understand how your superego reinforces its control. We alluded to it earlier in talking about how your superego gives you default cues for confusing situations.

Think back to your young life, between the ages of five and eight. Think about the mother or dominant mother figure in your life at that time. What single behavior of yours rankled her most often? Something did. She had a pet peeve about your character. Did she repeatedly tell you to quit asking questions? To stop showing off? To settle down? Or did she shake her head when she caught you daydreaming? When you spoke without thinking? When you got your clothes dirty? When you sassed her?

Find one and only one such general behavior that she frequently corrected. You might not get it right the first time. That's all right. The exercise still works.

Now go back to the same period of your life and think about your father or dominant father figure. What behavior tickled him the most? What got his attention in the good way? Was it showing off academically? Being a good sport? Making him laugh? Helping out? Being athletic?

Before I go on, I need to explain why you're noticing a lot of gender biases in this book. Gender biases – mothers expect this, fathers expect that, a proper family has one mother and one father – are of questionable value, of course. But they are soaked into the dominant rules of most current national cultures, with varying consequences, most of them terrible. Superegos are insistent on upholding or reacting unfavorably to the dominant cultural restraints. Either way, an individual superego is defined by those cultural biases. Superegos, like justice systems, are conservative by nature, highly resistant to change, and will use gender biases to belittle you even if you don't believe in those biased stories. I can't apologize for the ways of the parasite, but I do apologize if reading about *its* gender biases causes you hurt feelings.

Let's say that you have found two strategies for getting the approval of adults – for most people, one for men and one for women – and avoiding their disapproval when your understanding of what is going on is hazy. If it's a woman in charge, and you have a female caretaker who likes you to be quiet, you will look at the woman quietly. After all, it's what settles your maternal figure down, right? If it's a man in charge, and the voice in your head reminds you that your male caretaker likes to be entertained, brighten up and put on a silly face. After all, this new man is more likely to give you positive attention, right?

What's the point of a child having these two default strategies, one for women and one for men, when they're entering confusing circumstances? The default behaviors increase the chance that the child will draw the empathy of the adult, and they *buy time*. Instead of the freeze of panic or the instinct to run away, the child can stand on his or her two feet and wait a little, enough time for another cue to arise, or for the adult to signal more clearly what is wanted.

It turns out that there's a long, but limited, set of default strategies that superegos enforce. If you're still looking for yours, see whether any of these common ones apply to you. Any of them can apply to men or women and reflect the expectations of a father figure or mother figure, but one or two are likely to resonate more strongly with you:

I need to be more ladylike
I need to man up
I need to be tougher
I need to be less bouncy
I need to be funny
I need to stay quiet
I need to put others before me
I need to not be so full of myself
I need to stop taking pleasure from other people's misfortune
I need to hide
I need to stop being a smarty-pants
I need to give people things
I need to be a team player
I need to entertain others
I need to excel
I need to be perfect
I need to distrust other people
I need to be nice all the time
I need to stop being mean
I need to be smart
I need to stop fighting back
I need to hide who I am

Chances are, you have one of these defaults for women, and another for men.

Oddly, your two defaults never change, and they never depart through your entire lifetime. You don't get a better set. You're stuck with your two. By the time you're twelve, you've learned other strategies to gain the trust of adult men and women. By the time you're seventeen, you've learned *all* the other strategies. Read the list again now, stopping at each one and to ask whether you haven't used that strategy in one circumstance or another in your life.

So, shouldn't the superego pipe down and let you pick your strategy from the long list? Once you're an adult, don't you get to find your own way into an encounter with a stranger, without Mom or Dad or another caregiver lurking over your shoulder? You would think so.

Unfortunately, that's not most people's experience. All my clients, for instance, tell me that when they're intimidated by a new circumstance – a blind date, or a change in boss, an unfriendly cashier, or a robotic customer service agent – they default to their oldest strategy. Why? Because their superego is in charge. The helpful parasite doesn't retire at twelve or seventeen. It remains in command, quietly whispering to the grown-up Jade as if she's still seven years old.

To our superegos, Jade and you and I never grow up. In a way, the parasite's messaging reinforces my sense of acting through an inner child, the kid who still seeks adult protection, even though my body and mind are mature and evolved.

Which brings me to the matter of the superego's obsessive incessance. At six or seven it takes charge. Pretty soon after that, it runs the show all day long, every day, and for nearly every significant decision that the human being inside experiences. You think you have been running the show, but you haven't. If that's news to you, read on. This book is about first proving that your superego shackles you all day long, and then helping you find your way free.

In the meantime, listen for its voice. The more you pay attention, the louder it is and the easier for you to hear it. Just listen for it. Don't complain or do anything about it. When you catch its inflection, stop for a second and label it. "That's my superego." That's all you ever have to do.

It was hard for me to pick out my superego at first. Lots of thoughts ramble around any old mind, most of them fragments, some of them strategies, lists or observations, and a few that respond accurately to challenges. Mixed in are the superego messages. They are prominent during conflicts. If you feel urgency and danger, and there isn't a literal snake coiled in front of you, then you're bound to be in the realm of the superego. Usually, you don't notice the urgency and danger consciously. You react first. By the time you hear your superego, it's offering its wrap-up comment: "You idiot." "I can't believe you did that." "What? Again?" "Loser." Some superegos come right out and say those things. Others are harder to hear, but their snarkiness and contempt are evident. Whether you hear it call you a name like "loser" or just leave you with a sense of disappointment, take the time to stop and say, "That's my superego." Identify it. If you want, you can add "I don't deserve that," but don't get into an argument with it. Just label it and move on. The point here is to start to develop an awareness of its presence, and its voice if you can hear it. As a vampire, it prefers the shadows.

The more you notice it, the more you get to know it. It does not want to be known, because it can't compete with your adult sophistication. It knows that it's easily the dumbest kid in the classroom, and the dumbest voice in your head. Elsewhere you may have an adult teacher in you, but you're taking your cues from a back-row bully.

You might make out its voice once a day at first, or as little as once a week. But the more you pay attention, the more often you'll hear it. For most people, it pipes up hundreds of times a day. If you can notice it five times in 24 hours, you're a master at this exercise.

SIX

GROW UP AND RELAX

Fifteen years ago, I was in my therapist Robert Birnbaum's little office cottage behind his house in Lafayette, California. I was trying to deal with my issues: my inglorious past, dogged shames and regrets, unlovability and worthlessness. The usual mess. A gremlin popped up on my left shoulder and without a thought I started talking to it. It talked back. Everything in this book stems from that chance occurrence. My gremlin – a rat with wings and a longer, toothier face than a bat – was a physical representation of what Freud called my superego. That gremlin accompanied Robert and me for a once-a-week, six-month wild ride through my defenses, my identities, and my litany of anxieties. It was a dizzying, stubbornly crass and narrow trip as I first tried to stand up to my gremlin, then argue with it, and finally just let it show itself until it was satisfied that I had grokked its messages. I learned that it was simple-minded, crafty and mean-spirited, but honest (when I ask it a question, it answers honestly). But mostly I learned that it would disappear the more I let it be seen. By the time I stepped away from studying the gremlin – after about six months of once-a-week encounters – my life was more peaceful and much more satisfying.

Ten years later, in 2017, as I focused my growing coaching practice on helping clients tame their own inner critics, the gremlin experience was prominent in mind. So, I tested whether it could be replicated with others, and discovered that it was the easiest thing in the world for anybody to meet their own superego. I also discovered that engaging one's superego directly, as I had in Robert's cottage, might have the same therapeutic benefits for others that it had for me.

This book is based on my experiences with hundreds of clients over the past four years, as well as similar engagements with friends and relatives who asked about "my little parlor trick," as I referred to it. It's easier to accept a parlor trick than an encounter with one's own superego. This book is then a description of events I have witnessed. My intention is not to contribute to the academic or scientific understanding of the forces of the mind, but to show people some techniques that are as simple as parlor tricks but seem to offer a path to wisdom. I experienced some changes in attitude as I allowed myself to be guided by spiritual and psychological teachers. Afterward, I backtracked to figure out the mechanics so I could refine what I learned and deliver it to others. But as far as I'm concerned, deductive reasoning adds only a little to doing the work. That said, I'm not unaware that this book may seem to contradict some standing theories and would require double-blind testing to be trusted by anyone with a rational mind. Fundamentally, and probably most controversially, it breaks apart Freud's brilliant tripartite unconscious mind. In seeing the superego as a subconscious interior force, Freud wove it tightly into a system that required an understanding of castration, penis envy, the Oedipal (and now, Elektra) complex, and a general sexual orientation to its beginnings and its manifestations. My clients and my experience indicate to me that the superego is not an interior force at all, but a late-arriving parasite that isn't at war with the supposedly impulsive *id* – your survival and libido instincts. It operates as an independent being and has its own structures that stand apart from everything about me that is inborn, including my id. I don't expect anyone to believe this right off the bat, but instead of it being subconscious, the superego may simply be subvocal. It whispers, from the outside, usually slightly behind one of your ears. One nice but unintended consequence of this would be that the patriarchal biases that get poor Dr. Freud into so much trouble are unnecessary with this formulation of the superego. It's the same superego for men or women, and it's not a response to the fear of castration.

Robert Birnbaum passed away in 2012, and I never got a straight answer from him whether the Gestalt I enjoyed for those six months with my gremlin was something he commonly evoked or instead emerged organically in our sessions. But either way, I imagine that Robert's having studied directly under Fritz Perls, a father of Gestalt Therapy*, and Carl Rogers, a father of positive psychology, had something to do with the life-affirming, self-optimizing Gestalt experience that I'm bringing out into the world. By Gestalt, I just mean adopting two voices and fabricating a conversation between the two. Usually, Gestalt involves imagining an actual person you're in conflict with; here, the person is replaced by the belittling parasite who talks to you all day. You play the role of your super-ego and its questioner, alternately.

Now back to the task at hand: using these methods to relax your own superego.

Your superego doesn't cripple you just by defaulting to a sim-ple-minded strategy. It's worse than that. Before the parasite has presented its solution, it has cleverly removed most of your choices. It scares you,

---

*When I use the term "Gestalt," I'm talking only about a single technique that Gestalt therapists often use, in which the client faces an empty chair and pretends another person, often a mother or father, is sitting in it. Then the patient alternates roles, switching to the "mother" chair when responding to the "child's" question, and vice versa. The conversations I had with my super-ego reminded me of my experience with Gestalt role-playing. The longstanding central text for Gestalt theory in practice is *Gestalt Therapy* (Gouldsboro, MA: Gestalt Journal Press 1951, 1994) by Frederick Perls, Ralph Hefferline, and Paul Goodman. My experience with Gestalt Therapy is limited to its empty-chair or two-chair role-playing exercises.

sending an urgent danger signal that instantly transforms the mildest interaction with the world into a substantial threat. Being on the defensive limits your choices to the conservative ones that your superego prefers. Your superego parasite is a fearmonger. It's *your* fearmonger. Most of what you know about fear you have learned from the parasite. All day long it tells you ghost stories, points out that you're anxious, mocks you for carrying childish fears, and subjugates you to its will. If not for the interference of your superego, far more of your interactions with people would seem benign or even pleasant.

Remember, the superego is civilization's response to living among strangers in a world of distrust and hierarchy. If your birthright clan isn't surrounding you and protecting you, you might be helpless in a treacherous world of strangers. You might, in fact, be in their territory where they have every right to kill you.

How in the world does it succeed in turning the relatively benign, civilized world into a constant threat? Mainly by appropriation. It steals its manners from the instinctual survival center, Freud 's id.

As you've seen, the superego is a facsimile of a person, with the attributes of voice, persuasion, and judgment. It's a created being. You created it in a sense, but the fact that we all get one, and that yours is generally about the same as everybody else's, indicates that the species has somehow embedded it in your development plan. So don't spend too much energy blaming yourself. As far as I can tell, none of us had a choice, or a chance.

Whether the superego has learned how to behave from looking around, or has some embedded wisdom, it's pretty clear from the language that we use that it stole some of its persuasive powers from the id. Instinctual fear of death is immediate and urgent. When trapped or otherwise threatened with physical harm, the human organism reacts energetically, from nerves to muscles to brain in all sorts of sudden and chemical ways. With scarcely any lag time, the body fights, flees, or freezes. All attention is tuned to the physical danger. Often, time slows, strength and mental computation skills grow, and the body adjusts to best defend itself. Reaction is swift and targeted.

But when the danger is not physical, the body doesn't have an urgent reaction mechanism. Adrenalin doesn't flood in. The human organism doesn't automatically transform itself into a physical defender or a defender of any sort. When my boss looks at me sideways, nothing of my body chemistry signals that within moments my job will be lost, my life broken. But something subtly thinks that and pushes that message my way. A non-emotional outsider would say that at worst, I miscalculated what my boss wanted and one day might want to ask him about it. But my superego wants me to learn from my mistake, and its only reinforcement tool is the voice that punishes me verbally. How can it punish me if I'm objective about the importance of the minor infraction? My superego looks over at the id and sees how the id can get me to change my very chemistry by reacting to a danger with immediacy and urgency. If my survival were at stake, I would react immediately. My survival isn't at stake, *but my parasite tells me it is*. My superego tells me a subtle lie, that the danger is real, now, and my response must be swift. Now them's some big motivators for action.

The superego fakes me out, acting as if my survival instincts have been triggered. It borrows the survival instinct's notions of immediacy and urgency and applies them recklessly to everything that happens during the day.

From the first "uh-oh," I'm in its grip. Whether I've been stood up by a friend, overcharged by a repair shop, dressed down by a boss, or complained to by my partner, my very first reaction dooms me. My superego tells me I'm under attack and need to fight my way out right away. It focuses on getting out of trouble before I've even had a chance to take a good look at the circumstances. Nowadays, this is called "being triggered." You might think that just means an identity has been poked at, but the exact same feelings happen every time you believe that you are in danger. The superego responds the same way no matter what the threatening content.

Here's what shows up: Urgency. Need for immediate correction. Rising hackles. Defensive posture. Frown. Narrowed eyes. A pseudo-adrenalin charge in the spine. Whether I've just noticed my own blunder or I've been yelled at or the unexpected bill has arrived, it's the same. The superego has successfully taken over.

Think about the times when you've handled a minor conflict well. What did you do? You took a breath and looked around. You put it in perspective. You laughed to yourself. You stayed objective. How often have you handled a minor conflict well, right from the start? If you're like most of us, hardly ever. Instead, you've been prodded by your nasty parasite to jump to a conclusion of urgent danger, and you've rushed to judgment and action.

What possible good could come from such behavior? Why would everyone have evolved to jump to conclusions and harsh judgments rather than stand back a little and reason with the situation? It turns out that the superego has a method to its madness of urgency and catastrophic thinking and that overall, it serves the species pretty well, even while it subjugates us to a living purgatory.

The thing about society is that it requires a status quo. Instead of relying on the natural order, which has no limits and politically would be considered anarchy, society creates a peculiarly human order that is outlined in what we call morals, ethics, rules, and laws. Natural law allows; human law limits. Those limits create a not-quite-natural order, and they need to be enforced and maintained. Natural law doesn't have what we call judgment; before Adam and Eve ate of the tree of knowledge, good and evil didn't exist in God's universe. One of the drawbacks of being human, it turns out, is that we have judgment of good and bad, right and wrong. The more stable our collective notions of what is just or unjust, the more likely that our society's grand plans – building highways, signing treaties, getting everyone to worship once a week and preferably on a particular day – will be carried out. Yes, there's a subtle agreement between most notions of justice and natural or biological law, but that's a far cry from declaring any ethical system to be incontestable or unchangeable. Human law is expedient, and one of its central characteristics is stability and the maintenance of a status quo. Except in the occasional crises, human laws change little and slowly. Human laws protect a status quo. In that way, they are essentially conservative. All sorts of impediments are put in the way of changing laws.

As the personal enforcer of my society's morals, ethics, rules, and laws, my superego is exactly as conservative as my society. My parasite is a stickler for the status quo. It enforces the rules it has already learned and responds to any equivocation on my part with a metaphorical whack to the back of my head. Forget situational ethics.

The rules that it has already memorized it wants applied. And here's where the true genius of its borrowing urgency and immediacy from the id comes into play. But to understand, first I need to explain something about how events arise within our consciousness.

We all have experiences. An experience can be as little as a thought: "Oh, look at that ugly dog." Or it can be as much as an accomplishment: "It took me three weeks to carve this pistol out of soap." Whether the experience takes a few seconds or a few weeks, it starts out the same way. Every experience starts with curiosity. You might think that curiosity is a big deal, since it can kill cats, but it's really not. It's just the beginning of every experience. Every moment, event, strategy, conflict, challenge, observation, project, thought (you get the picture) starts with a simple scan of the available variables. We start every experience with a relatively open-minded pair of questions: "What's here?" "What do I need?" The "what's here" part is a scan. If I'm a gardener, I first survey the plants for signs of change. I might sort what I'm seeing into loose frameworks – plants that are wilting, ones that are thriving, and ones that need pruning. I haven't decided what I'll do yet. I'm just collecting data for a while. If I've tentatively decided to read *Crime and Punishment*, I might open it to check how many pages it has, how big the type is, and, having glimpsed a few multi-syllabic Russian names, leaf to the front to see whether there's a handy cast of characters. I'm casually checking "what's here," so my known variables of time, attention span, eyesight, and memory can be brought to bear in my decision whether to read a 565-page crime novel. I'm collecting data.

When I get in my car, I check the instrument panel to make sure one of my kids hasn't run the tank down to empty. I'm collecting data. Curiosity equals collecting data. I keep collecting data until I think I'm juggling enough variables to either proceed to a conclusion or to decide whether to take up a particular kind of experience. Once I've got all the data that I think I need, I proceed to the next step of my experience, which is its execution. I won't go into execution here. We're going to stick with the curiosity stage, because that's where our parasitic superegos exert almost all their efforts. By the way, the third and final stage – completion – grants the experience meaning. We select a puzzle from the variables in front of us, work through the puzzle, and when it's solved call it a meaning. We're meaning-making machines! After which, we start all over again, collecting data with our playful curiosity for the next moment or event or project.

The most fun part is usually the first part, the initial curiosity, and its collection of data. From moment to moment, thought to thought, project to project, we get a kick out of selecting variables for the next puzzle and the next puzzle and the next one, so we can find a solution that traces a meaning, and then another meaning, and then another one.

Spending time in the first "what is here" stage is bubbly. As spiritual teacher A.H. Almaas points out, curiosity – the "what is here" stage – is synonymous with what we call "joy." Every moment, event, or project has its novelty, and with it, the surprise that comes from scanning a room, picking out toys, and starting to play.

Not to the parasite watching over me. My superego is a killjoy.

It cuts off my curiosity. How? Here's its genius. By creating a false sense of danger and urgency for correction, it sharply curtails my exploration of "what is." Instead of letting me scan the situation, and discover on my own what is what, my parasite jumps to a conclusion. Its default rule is presented as my chief if not only option. And because it has impressed me with a sense of urgency, my superego concludes the scan and proceeds to action. And so, I have not been allowed to slow things down and see whether I've missed something in the room – another option or another view of what is being said to me – and I respond the way I always have.

Ask yourself this: How much do I value being *first* to the answer? If I have been trained by my teachers to be the kid in the front row raising her hand breathlessly, "Ooh ooh I know I know!" – then I've given my parasite all the power it needs to cut off debate. The superego revels in being first to the solution and stopping me from meandering my way to another way out of the puzzle or the conflict. My superego has rigged it so that its conservative, rule-bound voice will always be first to the answer.

Imagine that your first "what is" scan that starts any experience has a range of solutions that are lined up in order from riskiest to safest. Your superego will always default to the safe region. The safest response is defensive and conservative. All of your creative, wild, risky possibilities are wiped out in an instant. You don't get to even see them, because your superego has already jumped you to a conservative conclusion. Maybe the superego is right, and this isn't a time to take a risk, but don't you get to decide that for yourself?

Want to test this? Take a beat and see what happens. Next time you step into a surprise conflict with your boss or partner or friend or family member, as your hackles rise and you find your lips starting to mouth a defense, stop. Wait a few seconds and look around. Ask yourself what else is in the room or in your antagonist's words or motivations. See if you've missed anything. Just by slowing down, you've usually defused things a bit. You've removed urgency and you've restored the possibility of objectivity, of taking a risk and not responding the way you always have in the past. It's cool, but it's not magic. You may still piss off the person you're in conflict with the first few dozen times you take a beat. But eventually, you might notice the default approach of the superego has started to wear thin (and wear off). You might even find yourself compromising and agreeing more often and noticing that most threats are fake. And just possibly the world might begin to feel like a safer, gentler place, which might be the loveliest change of all.

SEVEN

TAME THE PARASITE

Enough explanation. Let's agree that we have a rudimentary idea of how our superegos keep us in their thrall. Now where were we in taming the sucker? We left off from two exercises: First and foremost is the continual job of noticing it in action. Every time I notice my superego telling me I'm deficient, I have the opportunity to question its accuracy. All I have to do is say, "Oh, that's my superego," and I have introduced the possibility that its point of view is skewed. Its point of view is *always* suspect. Second is to engage in direct and sustained dialogue with the parasite. We'll suggest some prompts, but you always have the power. You can decide for yourself what you want to talk to the superego about. It's your body and your self, and you probably know best what is getting in your own way.

As you get better at hearing it, you might notice that the superego addresses you as a pathetic, helpless child. You're not. You're a fully developed adult. But you and everybody else let a superego infantilize you. Worse, the parasite doubles down on the claim of immaturity with further admonishments that you are essentially deficient, worthless, and unlovable. Don't take my word for it. Summon your own superego – pull it out from where it's hiding and sit it facing you at eye level – and ask it yourself.

"Do you think I'm capable of running the show without you?"

You can guess how most superegos answer that one. Negatory, with an eye roll.

Follow up with: *"How do you know if you don't ever let me?"*

Typically, the superego will respond by relating a story of failure, such as, "Just look at how you crashed and burned as a sophomore in college." Or "I guess two divorces aren't enough." Or "What about the mess you made of your last job?"

Respond with, *"But you were running the show then, weren't you? So, isn't that on you?"*

Most superegos go silent at this point. Some will test their host with more examples or a stubborn refusal to take credit for failures. Don't get frustrated. Stand your ground. You have the right to be in charge. Inside, you can pity the superego for being so scared of change. But outside, show it respect. You want to avoid the bully/victim cycle that has always been its playground. If your superego continues to be mulish on this point, just flip it off mentally and go on to the next bit of dialogue.

"Let's agree that we don't really know what it will be like for me to take charge. That was then. This is now. You agreed to the experiment the last time we talked. I know it's hard for you. You have years of being in charge. So again, will you step aside so I can take charge for a while?"

By acting as if it has superior maturity and knowledge, the superego questions its host's value. From the viewpoint of the superego, a child has no current social value. A child is helpless and unproductive. The superego is only interested in productivity; activities of introspection and play are considered a waste of time. Value, from the superego's view, is externally derived. Your productive role in society is all that matters. The superego throws around the insults "lazy" and "procrastinator" to reinforce its view of value and associates them with immaturity.

Do you berate yourself for being lazy? Watching too much TV, maybe? Or for procrastinating? Putting off the vacuuming for one more day? Indulge me and think for one second how weird that is. What's morally, ethically, or legally wrong with wanting to watch TV and amusing that desire? What's morally, ethically, or legally wrong with waiting another day to vacuum? Yet just about all of us agree that sloth is one of the seven deadly sins.

If you listen closely to your superego, it frowns every single time you choose TV over housework or daydreaming instead of putting your nose to the grindstone. It has no balance. It is a rabid zealot, a dumb, repetitive rule-monger. If you are not being productive, you are worthless. You are being childish. You are only worth as much as you provide for society. Your value is your work.

What a drag that would be if it were true. How could we enjoy life if not for our simple, unproductive fascination with the wild, colorful world?

As your superego adopts and passes to you the rules of society, one after another, it provides you with guides to productivity. They are hierarchical ladders of worth. We call them identities. Anything that gets put at the end of the sentence "I am ..." is an identity. Here are some common identities: mother or father, son or daughter, worker, student, vegetarian, cisgender, non-binary, athlete, leader, follower, Christian, Muslim, friendly, tough, swimmer, lazybones, nature lover, spiritual seeker, and on and on and on. Each comes with its own socially enforced scale. Am I a good mother or a bad mother? Hardly anyone rates herself an average mother; just about every mom wants to be a top-flight mother. Am I a sandlot athlete or an elite athlete? Am I brilliant at loving nature or just OK? And then I pick at myself: How many species of native trees can I name? How many nights have I camped in the backcountry? *Everything* is on a scale.

We live in an age of identities. Which side are you on in the culture wars? The political party wars? How much value do you ascribe to identity politics? As a woman, where do I rank in society? Where should I? Do I have a responsibility to tell off carnivores in my family? How nice a car should I buy? Must it be electric or is hybrid good enough? Do I have enough social media followers? These are fraught questions. Your super-ego seizes on them and uses them for its nefarious purposes.

To my way of thinking, our toughest spiritual task is to shift the defensive force of identities out of the way. Most of the work of my ego is engineered to raise and maintain identities. Most of my self-hatred derives from the inability of said identities to provide me with peace. In fact, they do the opposite. My structured identities require constant maintenance and addition, and all of them separate me from others. They may create circles of trust, but at the same time they reinforce distrust of all the many more people outside the temporary circle. Identities grant me mirrored associates at the expense of excluding all others. My identities are under constant threat from the outside world and require my earnest vigilance and best protective gear.

Most of us, though, believe that our identities are who we are, and are integral to our movement through the world. Wouldn't I turn into a boring, disliked blob if not for my identities, the things that I show off to the world?

Here goes: In my own case, in no particular order I'm an educated writer, father, husband, brother, son, carnivore, contemptuous know-it-all, cisgendered male, music lover, aesthete, gardener, narcissist, spiritual coach, seeker, cook, car owner, leftist, reader, lazybones, cyclist, and San Francisco Giants fan. Each of the nouns and adjectives is an identity I carry with me. I can tell because I can end the sentences "I am ..." or "I am a(n) ..." with any of these. You've got your own set. Most seem benign. But are they?

Let's take an example from everyone's favorite identity, the good mother, and see how twisted it becomes when put under a microscope.

Like most mothers, my client Margie frets over her maternal decisions. At fourteen, her daughter Amy has sprouted a muffin top that bulges out from a bare midriff. On the way home from the mall, Amy is silent and sullen. Apparently, Margie wasn't as subtle as she could have been in directing her daughter away from the midriff-exposure racks. "Stupid," Margie thinks to herself. "I'm just like my mother. I know I shouldn't shame my daughter, but I've done it. Now I have hurt her feelings, and it's all my fault."

The rest of the afternoon, Margie is caught up in her own hand-wringing. "This is bad," she thinks. "If I don't control this, Amy's self-esteem will fall. She'll start failing at school, probably do drugs. I wonder whether she's tried drugs already. I had at her age. I'm not a good mother. I'm not the type of mother a girl can confide in. I suck at this. I need help."

Margie needs help, sure, but not the kind she thinks.

The next day she calls me online for our weekly appointment. Her superego is in the shape of a red soccer ball that seems to have an eternal frown on its cartoonish face. She has been talking to it regularly at our sessions.

"OK, soccer ball," she says after pulling it out from behind her scalp. "Why do you think you need to tell me I'm a bad mother?"

"Because you are," it responds.

"I make mistakes, but that doesn't make me a bad mother."

"I didn't say it did," it says.

"So how does it help me to hear you tell me I suck at being a mother?"

"Because if I didn't, you'd make even more so-called mistakes."

"So, you don't think I can learn from my mistakes without you?"

"You never have."

"You've never given me the chance to show that I can."

"So?"

"So, remember our deal. You're supposed to step aside for a while and see what happens when I run the show without your snarky punishment. If you think I'm a bad mother, for instance, I want you to keep it to yourself. Will you?"

Red soccer ball is silent.

"I need an affirmative yes from you."

"OK."

"No, that's not good enough. I need a yes. I need you to mean it. You'll step aside."

"Yes."

"Thank you. And thank you again for saving my life when I was a kid."

Obviously, Amy should not be made to feel shame for having grown fat. We live in a time when the culture is playing with that possibility; mothers learn the latest correct procedures to follow in talking to their daughters about beauty standards. We will ignore here that some rules change at a dizzying pace. But we all agree that fat-shaming is bad. What's less obvious but just as true is that Margie should feel no shame for having hurt her daughter's feelings. Moreover, she shouldn't feel shame for being a flawed mom. We all hurt each other's feelings, and all moms are flawed moms. At worst, Margie made a tiny mistake in the store. At worst, her daughter recognized again that adults enforce a lot of social expectations on children. Let's give mother and daughter the benefit of the doubt. A mistake isn't a sin. And hardly any mistakes lead to catastrophic disasters. The hoary proverb "For the want of a nail, the shoe was lost; for the want of the shoe, the horse was lost ..." is never how wars are decided or how the world actually works.

As a child learning the rules, you're going to get things wrong a lot. Your ability to predict consequences of actions hasn't been refined. But by eighteen, almost everybody is good enough. We're all 80 percenters, as the writer David Roche points out in his lighthearted "Church of Eighty Percent Sincerity." We get it right 80 percent. That's enough. The 20 percent we fail at – through ignorance or stubbornness or, most likely, failure to notice a conflicting variable – is never deserving of shame. It's just the humbling reality that we're not anywhere near perfect at predicting the future.

Does Margie think on the drive home from the mall that she is an 80 percent mother who is bound to get it wrong sometimes? Absolutely not. Why not? Because her red soccer ball doesn't let her. By inventing a ridiculous scenario of catastrophic consequences resulting from mistaken behavior, Margie is incessantly introduced to shame. In addition, red soccer ball reinforces a rule that Margie is not allowed to hurt her daughter's feelings. Good moms don't hurt their children's feelings. Bad moms do. Over and out.

Everybody gets hurt feelings. Margie on occasion hurts her daughter's feelings. Amy on occasion hurts her mother's feelings. Usually – not always, of course – a hurt feeling is an overreaction to a mistake or a misunderstanding. The person with the hurt feeling can't give the so-called attacker the benefit of the doubt. Regrettably, everybody is always doing the best that they can, and all of their so-called attacks are rooted in worrisome defensiveness. But the superego, which is a rule enforcer, gets in the way and assigns blame. This is necessary in society to get things done, presumably. Infractions deserve shame, or at least negative reinforcement.

But what exactly is a hurt feeling? How can a feeling, which has no substance, be "hurt," a word whose etymology is the butting of a ram or stag? The superego as usual borrows physical, survival language and imposes it on me. Now I have the pretense of a physical pain, somehow transferred magically to a bundle of possible emotional states I have stored in memory. What kind of alchemy is this?

Ultimately, Margie may want to ask her red soccer ball why it doesn't let so-called hurt feelings glance off. Why does it use words like pain, hurt, and wounding for ephemeral thoughts that carry no physical sting? Before I offend your sensibilities even further, let me add a few cautions. First, mean words are no good. Being mean is no good. Being non-empathic is no good. I totally agree with you about that. Also, it may well be that there are times when bad emotions lead to bad physical outcomes: failure-to-thrive theories, broken heart syndrome, and neurological studies tying emotions to physical responses are all the rage. Here, though, I'm talking about everyday, commonplace hurt feelings, the kind that lead to the nursery rhyme "Sticks and stones may break my bones, but words can never hurt me." I think we can all agree at least that words alone do not break bones. But we use words that are derived from physical states – "emotional hurt" and "emotional pain," for instance – as if we understand them as operating with the same mechanics as things that break bones, and they simply don't.

Let's take another example of how identities can be troublesome obstacles. There's a common rubric in our culture that one enters adulthood seeking fame, fortune, or power – or some mix of the three. Through a national mania for something called "leadership," school kids are all encouraged to set their sights on fame, fortune, and power.

My client Dave did well in English classes, all the way through high school. Teachers told him he was a "good writer." They said he was "talented." He won a school award. Writing became his thing; most high school students have "a thing." In college, he appropriately decided to concentrate on his thing. He studied writing and affiliated courses – literature, drama, psychology – and learned more and more. He accumulated practical knowledge and grew to see writing as not so much a talent as a perseverance through technical mastery. Like most of the tens of thousands of college writing students who graduate every year, his dream was to publish a novel or screenplay, maybe the Great American Novel or an Oscar winner. Novel-writing is a path to fame, like basketball or Hollywood or TV journalism.

After school, Dave got a job writing copy for an ad agency, making $45,000 his first year, and more than six figures after five years. He had achieved financial stability before he was thirty, and could look forward to finding a wife, having kids, and enjoying a house in the suburbs, a reliable car and a couple of nice vacations every year. The American Dream. It's the same American Dream, by the way, whether you're a new immigrant or a Mayflower descendant. And it's not just American. Standard of living is the one measurement of success that most countries have adopted as the end-all and be-all. It has superseded most other measures of happiness for most people in the world. This is good for the species presumably, but not necessarily good for the individual.

Is Dave happy about his choices? Absolutely not. His superego second-guesses him, continually. To address the uneasiness that he is left with, David employed the Gestalt method of having a conversation with his superego during our session together. He calls his superego "Chewy," because it looks like an unfriendly version of Chewbacca from Star Wars, all hair and snout. He pulls Chewy out from the back of his head and addresses him firmly but without anger.

"I'm single. I've saved some money. Why shouldn't I stop what I'm doing and write a novel?"

"That's a dumb idea," Chewy says.

"What's dumb about doing something I've always wanted to do?"

"Lots of things."

"Like what?"

"You're rising in your field. You don't want to throw that all away."

"I'm talking about dropping out for a while, not necessarily forever."

"Good luck clawing your way back in."

Dave thinks a second. "You're right. It might cost me a promotion, and I might have to step down a level when I come back. But I think that's worth it."

Chewy sneers.

"What makes you think it's not worth it?"

"I know you. You've wanted to do this for years, and you've never done it. What makes you think you'll do it now?"

"Good point," Dave says. "But I can't know if I don't try, can I?"

"Why haven't you tried before now? Because you'll fail."

"Actually," Dave says, "I haven't tried before now because you've constantly told me not to. The only one who seems certain that I'll fail is you."

Chewy says nothing.

"If I'm going to do this, I'll need your support. You have to stop telling me that I need to get back to my regular job and paycheck."

"Why would I do that? You're interested in a pipe dream, not reality. I'm here to keep it real."

"What makes you think you know better than me?"

"Because I'm realistic. What are the odds you'll finish a novel? And even if you do, what are the odds it will be any good? And even if it's any good, what are the odds that you will get it published? And even if it gets published, what are the odds that you will sell a thousand copies? And even if you sell a thousand copies, what are the odds you will get good reviews?"

"The odds are poor," Dave says, "on all counts. I'll give you that. But maybe I'll learn something about myself along the way."

"Maybe you will and maybe you won't. I can't support you in this ridiculous pipe dream."

Dave says, "I don't need your support. I just need you to get out of the way while I do it."

Chewy stares at him.

"I need you to let me make my own mistakes now, Chewy. Can you do that?"

Chewy looks up.

"Chewy, you need to agree to step to the side and let me do this without your warnings. Will you do that?"

Chewy says, "OK. It's your funeral."

"No, Chewy, I need a simple, positive affirmation that you'll get out of the way and let me run this show."

"Yes. I will."

"Thank you. And thank you for saving my life when I was a child."

That's all there is to it. Of course, Chewy won't shut up that easily. But over time, as long as Dave is attentive to Chewy's behavior and messages, they will become quieter and less frequent. Dave might even get his novel written.

EIGHT

FOLLOW YOUR NOSE TO FREEDOM

What would life be like without a superego? How could you live without an externalized conscience? Who would guide you through right versus wrong and good versus bad?

The superego likes to think it's the last word. By calling itself your conscience or ethical manager, it suggests that left to your own devices, you would be a worse person making poor decisions. But by what authority does it rule? By its own authority!

Anna's superego looks like a mean boss she once had, a nasty woman she renames Flo. Flo's voice sounds like Anna's mother. During a session, Anna interrogated Flo about her superior attitude.

"What makes you think you know better than me, Flo?"

"I've seen your screw-ups."

"But weren't you running the show when I screwed up?"

No response.

"Please answer me, Flo. Weren't you running the show when I screwed up?"

"You don't know what you're doing."

"Flo, you're avoiding the question. I need an answer. Weren't you running the show when I screwed up?"

"Yes, but you didn't listen to me."

"I'm not sure that's true, Flo. I doubt that you are always right."

"I'm more right than you," Flo says.

"That may be. But how can I know if I don't try to run the show myself?"

"You'll fail. I know you."

Anna's conversation with Flo is completely typical. Almost all superegos I have met have answered her questions the same way. The superego can't actually cite any higher authority for its knowledge or advice. The superego is a facsimile of a person, and it lacks the sophistication of self-reflection or ordinary intellectual analysis. It has learned to mimic social conventions accurately, and simply parrot them back repeatedly, without any concern for their origin, applicability, or necessity. By sticking with risk-averse rules, it can claim a record of general appropriateness, whatever value that may have. But it lacks any claim to authority and without that lacks any association with a greater sense of truth. It has an attitude of superiority that is backed up only by its own bullying ways.

By the time you were leaving high school, you had gained far more sophistication than any superego. You knew more, were able to reflect on life better than your superego, and you had absorbed all the important strategies for decision-making and communicating with others. You also might have tested a few of the rules and found that society was pretty good at enforcing its rules. A couple of speeding tickets will slow down a driver. You know the rules, and you know what happens when you break them. So why does just about everybody assign final arbitration to a deliberate bully?

The answer has something to do with the complications of civilization. Such weird behaviors as living next door to strangers and accepting a bit part in a giant societal machine require an abundance of rules. In particular, the machine requires a hierarchy – actually a multitude of hierarchies – and each imitates a biological pecking order but is much more time-consuming and demanding. And to get you to buy into the many roles and disappointing placements that a cultured life requires, the civilization had to find a way to suppress your personal enthusiasms and belittle you into abiding by the rules.

In particular, the culture through your superego has planted a myth in you that helps you believe that if not for your superego, you would fail. The myth is found in all so-called civilized cultures. It's a myth that goes beyond belittling you; it takes you into the realm of scaring the bejesus out of you. It's the "bad seed" myth.

As expressed to Christians and Jews alike in the Book of Genesis, with cognates in other religions, the idea is this: God created Adam and Eve in His own image, and everything went along fine – it was *all good* – while they were in their natural state. They didn't have a lot of rules. They lived simply, almost like children, just picking things up, turning them over, and exploring. It would have been a nice, non-self-reflective seamless world to them, with little if any need for memory or predictive capacities. Then one of them disobeyed the one rule – don't eat the apple – and all hell broke loose. But wait a minute. Adam and Eve were living like two-year-olds, right? And what toddler wouldn't try out the apple, especially if told not to? Kicking Adam and Eve out of Eden seems like a massive overreaction. Who would deprive their two-year-old of a happy future just because she touched the lit stove once? God must have been reacting not to a specific incident – the apple in question – but to an innate character flaw in humans that he was just waiting to be revealed. Otherwise, the story doesn't make sense. And when Augustine and other ancient Christian philosophers figured out the story this way, they invented the term "original sin". Since we're born tainted with original sin, we can't be trusted to our own devices. We need a cultural superego, presumably, and a personal version of that cultural superego, which at first was described as a universal conscience – say, the Ten Commandments – and in more recent centuries has evolved into something called a personal conscience. (Not that the term "personal conscience" makes much sense when you think about it.) Either way, it claims that we need a layer of internalized ethics, and because we have an alternative tendency to sin inside us, it has to be a snarky bully at times, threatening punishment if it doesn't get its way. Similarly, Freud posits the id as a potentially sinful center that needs a counterweight.

It is understandable that everybody buys these notions. They keep the trains running on time, presumably. But what if original sin, bad seeds, and suppression of evil are all mythological inventions? What if true nature, from the perspective of humans in their cultures, isn't engaged in moral wars but is fundamentally rigged to the good? Could you have broad-scale human cooperation, even sophisticated laws and rules and industrialized civilizations, without a need for superegos running the show for each citizen of that world?

It turns out that this isn't a utopian question. My clients and I, and many others, have learned that right and wrong, good and bad can be learned so well by children that at maturation a person can regulate decisions within human law parameters for the rest of their lives. Without resorting to a superego. They discover that they don't need an external voice reminding them what to do and what is right. If you're mature, you might not need a superego. And as for the so-called exceptions, those people who simply can't abide by the rules — due to mental illness or other conditions — their superegos are ineffective anyway. For the great majority of us who adopt cultural responsibilities, it turns out that as adults we are perfectly adept at running our own lives in a safe and sane way without a bully around.

For Anna, it took only a few rounds with Flo in Gestalt sessions before she started to feel more relaxed in her everyday life. The nag in the back of Anna's head was still around, but far less active. Flo didn't retire completely, but she was sometimes gone for whole days, and when she returned, Anna knew what to do.

"Oh, that's you, Flo," she would say silently to herself. "Thanks, but I don't need you right now."

Scientists can't seem to resolve whether hunger is an emotion or a sensation. Do I have a mental desire for food irrespective of what my body needs, or is hunger an instinctual trigger to get me to fill my belly? Or are the so-called pangs just the sensed feeling that accompanies an empty belly? Only civilized people with their nearby grocery stores could ask such questions. Before food storage became commonplace, the idea of three squares a day was ridiculous. Food was eaten as it arrived, gorged upon if plentiful, and rationed if scarce. Hunger would have been hunger – a common existential threat that signaled it was time to lean into the spears and go find a rodent or two.

As a civilized person whose survival needs are consistently met, I'm not that interested in my own hunger. Shipping lanes and trucked-in produce and beef mean I'm not dependent on the local weather and topography to protect my kin from starvation. But the opposite question does intrigue me: Is *satisfaction* an emotion or a sensation? Is it the mental pleasure of consequences going my way? Or is it the feeling of a full belly? What if all that I know about satisfaction is derived from my comfortably plush stomach? I'm not kidding here. Maybe every time I'm satisfied by a movie or book or partner or task, it's just my body announcing, "Thanks, I needed that hamburger," and recognizing that my belly's survival concerns have been met.

After working through your superego issues for a while, you might discover that it isn't *you* who are dissatisfied most of the time; it's your parasite. You might then start wondering about the whole notion of dissatisfaction. What does it mean? Where does it come from? Why can't I be satisfied all the time? Why is it so much easier to recognize dissatisfaction than feeling OK?

Check yourself right now. Do you need anything? I mean right now, in your chair or on your bed as you read this sentence. Not in an hour, right now. I can promise you the answer is no, you don't need anything this second. If you are reading this, you are not in imminent danger of death. When you attach the word "need" to something, it means you can't do without it. There's no getting around that definition. A "need" is not the same thing as a "want." If you "want" something, you haven't ascribed necessity yet. So right now, you may want something, but you don't need anything, and I would love it if you would pay attention to that. Let all the things you might want, but aren't necessary, disappear from your thoughts for a moment. Right this moment you are protected from the weather, you aren't starving, and you aren't being mugged at gunpoint. Your needs are met. For everybody in a civilized society, this fact of not needing anything is true for about 99.9 percent of the conscious moments of our lives. And yet instead of recognizing that we're 99.9 percent satisfied, we complain that life is constantly letting us down.

This is very weird if you think about it. Stop for a second. Do you need anything right now? Right this second? If you don't need anything right this second, why don't you feel happy, or at least satisfied, even for the blink of an eye that we're talking about?

Sadly, no one in Hollywood, on Madison Avenue, or in your immediate family will be reminding you this week that you're satisfied, the world outside is OK, or that you're fine as is. Such pollyannish pronouncements wouldn't be productive, according to the standard tropes that hard work and selflessness are good for you. It's also the only path known to your own personal parasite. As long as your superego is whispering little dissatisfactions, you don't have the space to notice how fine things are, right now.

How often are you restless? How many times a day do you think about doing something other than staying where you are? What would it feel like to take the world as it came to you, instead of constantly trying to manipulate it into a better, or more satisfying, surrounding? We're getting to the heart of the problem of self-improvement. Maybe it's not such a good idea. Maybe visualizing a better me or a more fortunate me or a more satisfied me is not worth the trouble. What if I'm just setting myself up for another round of dissatisfaction, when I discover that the new, blissful me wears off, too?

All I'm saying here is that it might be simpler and more effective to remove your blinders rather than exchange them for a rosier set.

In the mid-1990s I worked for a franchising company that eventually became the Wyndham hotel group. I was the public relations manager for Ramada Inns and then a generalist for the holding company, which besides low-end hotel franchises also owned car rental and real estate brands.

Wyndham was put together by a master-of-the-universe Wall Street guy named Henry Silverman. Without making a big deal about it, he managed the operations of this giant company in a manner that would have given heart attacks to every other CEO I have worked for. There was one overriding rule, and it was so imbued in the culture that it was unspoken: If someone asked you to do something, you simply did it. Sounds authoritarian, right? Except that "someone" could be a name and title on the organization chart above you, below you, next to you, or far, far removed from you. *Anyone* could ask me to do something, and I was expected to do it. It was remarkable. What Henry Silverman figured out that no one had bothered to test was that people are by nature fair. They know that after they have asked something of you, and you have delivered, you have earned an equal right to ask for something back. A natural *quid pro quo* system arises. Since it happens that the greediest people are also the stingiest, they learn quickly that they better not over-ask, because they'll generate a huge number of unwanted tasks for themselves. Wyndham proved that "Just Say Yes" works beautifully in a matrixed, corporate environment. I was probably about the 400th-most important person in the company at the time. Normally the lower ranks aren't allowed to talk to the CEO, ever. But in the Wyndham system, when I needed the CEO's sign-off for a PR piece, I didn't send it up the line to first be reviewed by my boss and his boss before a secretary screened it and decided whether to send it elsewhere or to the CEO's desk. I just got permission from my boss to fax it to Henry and got his signature back in less than 45 minutes. His fax machine sat next to his desk. He didn't care what came through it; he would answer it immediately. The flattening of the hierarchy succeeded only because the *quid pro quo* system had connected us in a fascinating web that we all took pride in. The system had no resistance in it and became supremely intelligent for some strange reason. It was absolutely the best-run, most self-correcting and lighthearted corporation that I have worked for, and I know more than a few medium to giant private and public corporations from the inside and out. Its genius was Just Say Yes.

Ten years later I was applying the same to my entire life, and it worked pretty much the same way. I required myself to say yes to anything I could, for six months. There was more friction in the system, of course, since I was the only one in on the scheme. My friends, fellow workers and family, plus the daily strangers who help fulfill my needs, didn't share my approach. They still deliberated and weighed the consequences of saying yes. But in the end, even that didn't matter.

You learn a lot about not weighing consequences by just arbitrarily answering yes to everything. For one thing, you can generally trust that others have about the same interests that you do, and so things will probably work out about as well as if you agonized over the choice. That's humbling. But I also learned that in the end the consequences just don't matter much. One conclusion to an experience is about the same as another. It's over and there's a new experience that has popped up. Part of the rigmarole of planning is a lot of time spent in postmortems. Saying yes all the time obviates the need for postmortems. It more or less throws caution to the winds. And it turns out that's safer than we think.

After my six-month trial period experimenting with always saying yes in my personal life, I took my foot off the gas, and allowed myself to say no again. The funny thing is, I say no far less of the time now than I did before the experiment. I learned to trust other people's ideas for me, and to let them more often decide how I might spend my time. In a way, I get to see my life through other people's eyes now, and sometimes that liberates me. When Annie asked for a rose garden while surveying the unkempt, wild property we bought six months into our relationship, I said, "OK, I can do that," without a second thought. I had never been a gardener and knew nothing about roses. But I liked saying yes, especially to Annie.

Four years later, I'm single-handedly tending more than 300 plants or groups of plants that include thirty or so rose bushes, a half dozen fruit trees, two young redwoods, several dozen perennial flower species sprinkled around, from fuchsia to birds of paradise to purple stock, and daisies and azaleas, swaths of tulips and gladioli and daffodils and other bulb flowers, tons of geraniums, rows of squat flowering bushes and tall grasses that form aesthetic barriers, legacy camelia and rhododendron bushes the size of trees, a number of poisonous oleander marking property lines, as well as wisteria crawling the fences front and back, which I likewise inherited, bougainvillea heading up one side of the house, two grass lawns, two large Japanese maples, a leggy walnut tree, an orange shock of wild California poppies, hundreds of bunched sprigs sprouting on the hillock behind the vegetable garden, three frighteningly delicate abutilon saplings, favorites of Annie's, a pair of grape vines on arbors, five or six herbs for the kitchen, as well as cherry tomatoes, Brussels sprouts and leeks, bushy clumps of Mexican sage and a scattering of low-lying native succulents and pansies, and did I mention roses?

If I had happened to say no when Annie casually asked for a rose garden, I wouldn't be spending an hour or two a day in love of plant life. And knowing Annie, someone else would be tending the rose garden, by which I mean a professional gardener. There was no compulsion for me to do it. She would have gotten her rose garden. I just said yes mechanically and figured that it would sort itself out later.

Following my nose is more of the same and goes well beyond just saying yes. Following my nose does not have an agenda. I do the next thing that shows up, seemingly out of nowhere, and it doesn't make any sense, and it can't work, and surely, I'll stumble into a rushing river and drown, and yet...

By simply following my nose, I'm neither disappointed nor particularly elated by what happens to me, with me, or around me. Whatever happens tends to enliven me. It's material, in the sense that a comic has material, and I can be fascinated by it no matter what. The next moment that comes is slightly unexpected, even if it's just noticing the right angles on my new office printer. Since I haven't anticipated much, whatever sticks out of the background and gets noticed seems to play out for me with little interference. I get it that I'm making decisions all along, both of what to pay attention to and of whether to get my teeth cleaned, but they're so light that they feel more like entering a game than making a consequential prediction, and I sincerely don't notice the decision until my calendar that day sends me to the dentist.

I'm lucky that I've never valued my time much. Doing one thing has about the same value to me as doing something else, even if the first is seeing a movie and the second is holding the hand of a dying person. This may sound crass to you, as if I don't value tenderness more than silly diversions. But I'm saying that I don't value *time* differently. If I'm in a silly diversion, I don't feel like that's wrong, or worthless. It's where I happen to be, and it is full of wonders of its own. The only period when I felt differently about the value of time was when I was actively raising children; anything that contributed to their health and welfare seemed worth more. But I've never bought into the idea that some activities are a waste of time, or a distraction. In fact, these days I believe that if anything, most of my productive life has been a distraction from investigation of the world as it really is. Neither is necessary. I don't expect to ever find a purpose, and I'm glad for that. I'm *productive* for the sake of the species – keeping human beings robust and spreading around. I *investigate the world* out of fascination – being drawn to truth for the sake of truth, and love for the sake of love. Nowadays I spend more time in the latter, and counterintuitively I'm also lucky enough to be able to incorporate truth and love in my productive life.

Part of following my nose is surrendering to the fact that all experiences, which means all thoughts and activities, have about the same weight. When I'm following my nose all the time, everything inside and outside seems light, almost feathery. The illusion of profundity disappears. It turns out that divine states of being, such as presence or non-dualism or the awesome feeling on top of a mountain, at least to me, are simpler and more permeable and easier to encounter and enjoy than familiar, duller socially derived states of being. I cringe a little when I hear gurus and teachers say, "Let's go deeper." While there's certainly a richness to spiritual experiences, they are also light as a feather.

I had to release a lot of defensive armor, I think, before following my nose could show up. Somehow, I had to trust that the interdependent river could carry me along with it safely, and that even if I didn't have a map, I could lightly steer while looking around and enjoying the ride.

NINE

CIVILIZATION AND ITS DISCONTENTS

We're all theologians. Every one of us. Think about it for a second. Have you ever met anyone not interested in the existence of God? Even an agnostic asks the question, "Why am I here? What is my relationship to existence? Am I just a random mistake, a cog in an impenetrable system, or does it matter how I live my life?" Most people want to live lives of purpose and value. For guidance, the atheists turn to human ideals and values, the religious to scripture, and the spiritual to gurus. They're all asking the same theological questions. What is my relationship to the universe (God), and what is my relationship to other humans (not-God)? What do I control, and what do I need to control? Theologians, philosophers, social scientists, and even physicists root their work in these questions. Mostly, they come up with the same answers. What hardly anyone bothers to notice is that the moral/ethical structures that have survived the world's globalization are all just about the same. After World War II, the United Nations came up with a catalog of conventional human rights – an ethical structure for nations – that only the most fanatical, outlying religions or spiritual movements would dispute.

Most nations signed on. In 1993 at the Parliament of the World's Religions, virtually all religions signed on to a similar ethical agreement. Apparently, the ethics game isn't all that difficult since just about everybody gets the same right answers.

You probably believe in the Golden Rule: Treat others as you would like others to treat you. Most of the rest of any ethical structure is subtext or exception-setting. I'm sure you learned the Golden Rule, and had it repeated over and over again, when you were a child. How many times did a parental type respond to your hurtful behavior with, "Would you like it if that happened to you?"

We think of ethics as necessary for humans to get along. But that might not have always been so. If we were still living in small, tribal pods instead of large and, now, industrialized civilizations, the ideas of fairness and justice might not be needed very often. Without private property, fairness doesn't show up. Without distrust, justice doesn't show up.

Humans for a long time probably didn't need a bunch of rules to protect property and mete out justice. In his book *The World Until Yesterday: What Can We Learn from Traditional Societies?*, the anthropologist Jared Diamond describes small tribal clans in Bolivia, Brazil, and New Guinea as operating without central authority or a formal justice system. There are conflicts and rules, but far fewer than we're used to. The great majority of bickering is over food sharing or adultery, which are interests of the *id.* And the great majority of gossip is over falling out of trees, predatory animals, scarce resources, and other survival issues, also interests of the *id.*

As the rules and possible conflicts built up in civilization, most of them covering conflicts quite remote from survival, so did the material for the superego to govern. If you're not in a Stone-Age tribe, and you have a roof over your head and a few meals stored in the refrigerator, the odds are that you're spending almost all of your life in the material of the superego, not the id.

With all those rules to keep track of, don't I need the superego to accompany me? Once I'm a product of civilization, isn't an externalized ethical voice my only protection from naively or maliciously breaking the rules? Not really, because by the time I'm seventeen or so, the superego already has prepared me for just about anything new to come my way. It did that by curating my memory, starting when I was about five, even before it fully took over. Now I know that you believe your memory and think that it tells the story of your life back to you. But what if a person's memory isn't an accurate recording of the events of a life? What if it is instead a book of moral tales, each of them concluding in a warning or a reward? Most are tales of fear and danger to be avoided in the future, with a few blissful ones telling us the reward if we quit making stupid mistakes. Our memories are our moral upbringing in retrospect, and the more important ones are all stored away before we're out of high school. From then on, they're available to us with or without a superego reminding us. They become the basis for our ethical pattern recognition skills. When we encounter an ethical issue – which usually involves arguing for what we want or giving in to what someone else wants – our minds have an answer pre-mapped-out in the relevant memory or memories. This all goes on without much notice, as it probably does in the other animals, albeit for them through association rather than cause and effect. Add in our critical thinking skills, and we've got a sophisticated apparatus capable of dealing with most decisions all by itself.

In addition, I'm probably bent to the good. Tribal people don't need fairness and justice systems because they haven't stopped defaulting to sharing and trust. Your typical three-year-old will give away her peanut butter sandwich at least twice before she realizes that she is left hungry. Besides sharing and trusting, we also probably default to compassion and empathy, and to perseverance and peacefulness. Overall, the human system that occupies my body most likely defaults to what we call "the good." My pre-moral self isn't immoral. I'm not a bad seed. Nor am I a blank slate. Quite the opposite; I'm pretty good by nature. Which isn't to say that by nature I'm infallible. Civilization presents daily conflicts as people packed into busy hierarchies try to get along with each other. By introducing toilet paper, civilization created the ethical dilemma of who replaces the empty roll. Like many everyday small behaviors, not replacing the roll can lead otherwise placid family members and roommates to anger and contempt. If I'm in conflict, I have a perceived need that is somehow blocked by someone else's perceived need – in this case, getting on with their day in a hurry, without bothering to replace the roll. Sorting these conflicts out is the primary task of human, culture-created rules. Most of the hard part of growing up is learning the rules. Yes, it's expedient to not replace the roll, but it's not fair to the next person. Would you like to be the poor creature without toilet paper? The superego assists in the work of learning the rules, through bullying and memory creation. By the time you are seventeen, its memory work is completed. It has locked in all the moral tales you might need. You get why the rules need to be obeyed, and you know enough rules. You can self-administer your ethical code, without bullying. The superego can be retired. You don't need it anymore; you can take charge.

My clients and I have tested this out. Life without an active superego turns out to be *more* moral and ethical and appropriate, actually, because I'm spending less of my time defending myself from false dangers. Fewer conflicts mean fewer ethical dilemmas. My mind's full capacity for creativity is freed up. It not only has the common sense to make the right choices; it is also more accurate in assessing dangers. Mainly, I stop seeing danger where there is none.

My client Daniel's superego looks like a squirrel. He begins a session by asking Squirrel, "Why are you still in charge?"

"Because you need me."

"How do you know I need you?"

"You would fail without me."

"But if you're in charge all the time, Squirrel, you can't know that, can you?"

Squirrel is silent. His expression is disdainful, eyes narrowed.

"Isn't it tiring running the show all the time?"

Squirrel's eyes widen into sincerity. "Yes, it is."

"Wouldn't you like to go into semi-retirement?"

"Yes, but you need me."

"Well, let's see about that. Remember how you promised to step out of the way for a while? I think it's working. You're around still more than I need, but less than you used to be. I'm not failing, am I?"

"No."

"Then why don't you recede a little more. I promise I won't annihilate you. Remember? You'll be around, just way in the background. When I need you, I'll ask for your help. You'll be my Occasional Ethical Adviser. Is that OK?"

"I suppose so."

"Squirrel, I need a positive affirmation. I need a clear yes or no."

Squirrel responds begrudgingly, "Yes."

"I want to point something out to you. Remember when you first showed up when I was a child, your job was to help me learn the rules and mature. This is what you always wanted for me, for me to be an adult who could navigate the world on my own. So, your retirement means you succeeded. You should feel good about this."

"OK."

"Thanks again for saving my life when I was a kid."

"You're welcome."

Thanking your superego at the end of a Gestalt experience can be moving. Many of my clients tear up in appreciation as they are reminded of how their superego protected them as children. Gratitude is an essential feeling of the soul. It's the only essential feeling that looks back in time. The divine operates mostly in the present, with little concern for past or future. That's why so many spiritual movements emphasize "being in the moment." The unfiltered divine is accessible in the here and now. But there's one exception, and that's the aspect of the divine called gratitude. Appreciating the past as a series of influences and teachers, including your superego, is part of being rigged to the good.

TEN

WHAT, ME WORRY?

When I free myself from the superego, I'm also letting go of Mom and Dad and their counterparts. The superego is a simple-minded replica of my own mom and dad (or parental substitutes), in the guise of frowning and punishing judges. My superego belittles me, like parents have to when I'm first learning the ropes: "Listen, son, we know better." But by seventeen, I have outgrown the need to be belittled. My superego could have switched to conversing as a friend, I suppose, but there would be no point; my core self, the one inside that is already rigged to the good, has an observer of its own. One synonym for our built-in observer is *self-reflection*. It's also called *self-awareness*, and, in some spiritual communities, *awareness of awareness*. It accompanies all experiences and often looks like the fundamental instrument of consciousness. It can sound like a voice or not. Either way, it has its own curiosity and prowess in solving puzzles. It can draw on memory for patterns and discrete pieces of information. It is an adult. It doesn't need a mother or father for guidance, and it certainly doesn't need to motivate by bullying, belittling, and threatening punishment. It knows how to predict consequences, and also knows its own limits in predicting consequences. It can be trusted.

When Jade's superego first showed up, its purpose was to act like her parents when they weren't available. She could be alone walking home from school, and the hard-to-learn rules would be reinforced by the new voice in her head that acted like her parents. But Jade's superego never stopped acting like a parent who knows better and is ready to frown or punish if she slips up and forgets the latest rule.

Freeing yourself from your superego has the feeling of maturation. You lose the parasite that has spent most of its lifetime convincing you that you're a child and need a parental voice to succeed in the world. When you move the superego toward semi-retirement, you're giving a final heave-ho to your parents in a way. Mom's nagging voice or Dad's withering look disappear from your mind. Without them, you look down and notice that you're succeeding, and standing on your own two feet. That's the feeling of being mature.

My client Tracy calls her superego, which has the face of a cat, Tabby.

"You've been nagging me, Tabby," she says.

Tabby sneers, and Tracy remembers that she has to rephrase her concern as a question: "Will you stop nagging me, Tabby?"

"Why should I?" Tabby says.

"I don't need the nagging. At least ten times today, you have reminded me of a meeting tomorrow. It's on my schedule. I'm ready for it. I don't need to think about it until tomorrow. Why do you keep bringing it up?"

"You might forget it."

"That's not what I asked you, Tabby. I asked why you don't believe me that I can keep track of my to-do list without your constant nagging. If I thought about my to-do list twice a day, that would be enough, but you bring it up ten or twenty times a day, and never with a good feeling about it. Why don't you believe that I can run my schedule without your interference?"

"Because I've seen you mess up," Tabby says.

"Which proves nothing," Tracy says. "You were nagging me over and over and I still messed up. But that's not the point. I think I can run my to-do list myself. Will you quit nagging me?"

"No."

"No?" Tracy asks, incredulous.

Tabby smirks.

"I need you to quit running my to-do list, Tabby. You agreed to step aside, and this is part of stepping aside."

We all know that look from our parents when we've disappointed them or angered them. It strikes a position of authority and demands that we shrink or cringe. Every superego uses that memory to its advantage.

Belittling is a form of punishment in itself, of course, since as an adult I don't want to feel small and immature. Nagging is like that, too. Glowering is more direct punishment. We don't just listen to the superego narrow our choices in the moment. We also fear its future entrances, either through nagging or more directly punishing us with the rising chorus of embarrassment, guilt, and shame.

Embarrassment is the flush of "Oops, I made a childish mistake." Guilt is the claim, supported by the superego, that "I did something bad." Shame is the more dramatic claim, also readily provided by the superego, that "I am bad. There's something wrong with me."

Through nagging, glowering, calling me names, and demanding that I take on guilt and shame, the superego keeps me worried about the future consequences of my actions. Freud put it simply:

Anxiety is the fear of being punished by the superego.

The anxiety isn't from imagining that you might get the wrong answer or do the wrong thing. That's just the objective risk built into life. The anxiety is the fear of your own resulting self-punishment. You are cringing at the possibility of being bullied. You know the bully is coming, and you're seeking an escape route. The bully is always the same: a scornful look from a parental figure. This is worth knowing for two reasons. One, if you're feeling anxious, now you might be able to abstract its source – fear of being punished by the superego – as a way to start an objective inquiry into that particular anxiety. Being once removed from a fear – looking at it objectively – relieves some of the emotional burden instantly. Any suffering, including the suffering called anxiety, can best be softened by staying with it and inquiring into its qualities, hidden assumptions, and history. We complain in order to be rid of the complaint.

Second, knowing Freud's definition of anxiety might encourage you to work on retiring your superego. Do I need to be frowned at in order to act wisely? I can tell you that after six months of weekly encounters with my superego in therapy sessions, not only did it shift to the periphery most of most days, but my level of generalized anxiety dropped eighty-five percent. Don't ask me how I came up with a way to measure that. I just know that I was walking around with that much less anxiety. After decades of nighttime wakefulness and occasional insomnia, I have spent the subsequent fifteen years dropping to sleep in a minute or two most nights and waking up eight hours later refreshed. My wife asked me to remove that last sentence because it will cause people to hate me, especially lifelong insomniacs like herself. Because my superego work had such a dramatic effect on me, I decided to study it and refine what had happened to me into the methods that this book describes.

Some of my clients get substantial relief from anxiety after just a few interactions with their superego. For others it takes months or a couple of years. The effect varies, and it isn't always pronounced. Engaging your superego in a Gestalt is not a panacea for anxiety, but it ranks right up there with Valium.

ELEVEN

ENJOY BEING ORDINARY

Ten years after I met Bob Birnbaum and embarked on spiritual adventures, I found myself dating Annie – and her public. Her nineteen books, some of them sensitive novels and others inspired examinations of everyday suffering, are intellectually provocative, brilliantly thought through, and so plainly personal that many of her readers adore her as a refuge or invent a kinship with her as a secret friend. When Annie and I went out to the movies or restaurants together, I got used to being interrupted for a selfie or words of praise from a stranger. I learned to be the minister's wife – smiling, appropriate, quiet, and politely off to the side. I usually end up taking the selfie, since Annie's besotted fans are singularly uninterested in my handsome mug.

The message is clear: Annie is valued for her extraordinary talents. I'm ignored because I'm ordinary. Who wants to be around ordinary? Who wants to be ordinary?

I do. Annie does. You do. You might not know it, though.

Do you know how much easier life is when you're ordinary? If you're like most people, life is constant, repetitive reinforcement of identity structures. Your personality is like a garden or a home; it requires constant upkeep. My ordinary self? No maintenance required. My ordinary self isn't hierarchical, trying to be better or not be worse. It's OK with how things are, right now, more or less. Tasks are required, of course. Spirituality doesn't clean the dishes. But one task is the same as another. The task presents itself, gets done, is complete, and on to the next task. Writing this book, paragraph by paragraph, feels like doing the dishes, plate by plate. Hardly anyone bothers to measure my dishwashing. I don't have to measure my own writing, thank God. The same sentences get improved by my self-correction, what we call editing, whether I think I'm an ordinary talent, a genius, or a failure.

This is going to take a shitload of practice. Civilization trains us to be judgmental about just about everything, and to trust no one. But think about it. Whom do you trust more? The alpha dogs at work or the nice cashier at Safeway? Being around ordinary people is a relief. No one expects much of me when I'm talking about the weather.

Being ordinary isn't about not having wealth, fame, or leadership skills. Those pursuits, while often handicapping our access to empathy, are measured only within an external social structure. Justice and empathy operate in different realms. Most of us are obsessed with the justice realm, which nowadays focuses on standard of living. It is unfair that some people have vast wealth and others struggle for basics. That is a social problem that demands concern, work, and refinement. We vote, march, volunteer, and do our bit. At the very same time, our species has never been better at keeping down war, starvation, and disease. Over the same century that we've quadrupled our population, we've nearly doubled our longevity. For as far back as has been recorded, most individuals of virtually all cultures and tribes had an expected life expectancy of forty years at birth. Anthropologists believe this common life expectancy standard of 30-40 years may have stood since the beginning of humans 300,000 years ago. (Lifespan – the rough maximum that you or I might reach – is a different matter. It has hovered around 100 forever.) Expected life expectancy at birth is now closer to eighty in industrialized countries, fifty-five in developing nations, all that improvement coming in the past century. In India, median life expectancy has risen from a dismal twenty to a whopping seventy over the past century. The species is doing a very good job at refining its ability to grow and expand into new geographic niches, its primary Darwinian purpose. Which is not to say that this fantastic achievement doesn't have its unintended consequences. Global warming to name one. Yes, the world is unfair. Yes, the species is incredibly successful. No, the wealth of nations and the standard of living for adults aren't the only measures of success. In fact, they may be very poor indicators of individual satisfaction.

The Jesus who delivered the Sermon on the Mount to a disbelieving crowd would have said, "Duh." When this radical teacher said, "Blessed are the poor in spirit, for theirs is the kingdom of God," he pointed out that the world is exactly upside down, that the rich are worse off, and the poor are better off. How could that be? Aren't the poor to be pitied their poverty? If we're striving for a common and fair standard of living, sure. But there's an insidious discounting of the ability of people in lousy circumstances to engage in divine presence. Consider the possibility that at times at least, divine presence can be encountered separately from concerns of social justice, and maybe that's not a form of self-indulgence. Likewise, maybe a member of the hoarding class can let go of their beliefs in material value, at least for some time, and experience divine presence. Jesus didn't say that material possessions themselves prevent us from receiving grace; it's that focusing on their acquisition and maintenance takes our eyes off our own built-in kindness and generosity. Anyone wandering around the world with open eyes – even today – would notice that poor people are kinder and more generous with their goods and emotions than are rich people. Guarding wealth has its disadvantages.

If you're lucky enough to be poor in spirit in the Jesus sense – you have given up on the upside-down world of valuing riches, honor, and standing

– if you're so committed to being ordinary that you've abandoned all hope and help in achieving rank or being judged great, then you might have a shot at abiding presence. As you proceed through the course of life, you're nothing special, and then eventually you become nothing at all of any note. And then God or something else peculiar appears. Well, sometimes.

Hearing that, are you sure you want to be special? What if you could be unique – taking on the world with your own lens and individual expressions – without being special? What if being unique and being ordinary weren't at odds? While America doesn't encourage this view, you see it in Great Britain where the neighborhood eccentric is highly regarded. They're an ordinary bloke in all ways, but also an excellent painter of miniature soldiers, or cultivator of irises, or expert on Napoleon; they're a master of a socially useless province. We're all allowed to be that ordinary eccentric.

When I was a kid, all garbage trucks had a ground man, the guy who gathered the cans and pitched their contents into the hopper. Between stops, the ground man grabbed a handle at the back of the truck and slung himself onto a special step that carried him through the air as the truck traveled between stops. I've never seen a ground man not enjoying his work. The quintessence of all ordinary jobs, ground man on a garbage truck offers freedom, energy, outdoors, and simplicity. It's like bicycling. Who doesn't like the feeling of a bike ride? Who wouldn't want to ride on the back of a garbage truck? (You might need a nose clip the first few weeks.) I'm sure there is a mastery to being a ground man – conquering issues of safety, ergonomics, breath, speed, and accuracy. You don't want to slip under the wheels, and you want to clock out mid-afternoon. All tasks can develop into masteries, because we humans like to invent puzzles that can be perfected. But the freedom of the garbage man or bike rider isn't the mastery itself. It's their ability to do the job at hand and look around the neighborhoods that are passing by, enjoy the wind in their face, feel their pulsing heart. When you master something, you can take your attention away from it and be freed to be fascinated by other things.

If I don't have to be special, if I don't have to spend all my time maintaining a valued self-image, if I'm not worried about being judged, then I can discover how fun it is to watch the world unfold without having a stake in it.

If I'm ordinary, the judgments of others won't get in the way of my examination of the world at hand. If I'm OK as is, I can dawdle and day-dream and scan the horizon for hawks or bend down and investigate a roadside California poppy.

Presence – the mysterious essence that gurus and meditation teach-ers talk about arising when the obstacles of the superego disappear – is weird and distinctive at first. The idea of a point in time that doesn't need to be better, that can't be influenced much by me, that unfolds on its own as a spectacular vision that continues to the horizon? That's peculiar. We don't hear about spiritual *presence* in school; it has no obvious social value. It sounds supernatural, or as if I have to be as possessed as Joan of Arc to encounter it. But without warning or intention, presence starts to show itself to my clients as their superego defenses start to decline. They'll notice that the experience their superego wants to improve by going somewhere else is instead paused and allowed to exhibit itself. The pause creates a short reverie. It's like a meditation but more spontaneous and more eyes-wide-open. The world around them subtly transforms and exhibits odd phenomena that are distinct, describable, and common, albeit slightly abstract: stillness, smoothness, expansiveness, vividness, quietude, and sharp outlines that don't separate but exhibit a pervasive unity. Those are typical characteristics when entering what people call presence. It's pretty odd the first few hundred times it shows up.

The me who encounters presence has somehow freed itself, at least temporarily, from being an achiever or slob or handsome or ugly or young or old. The me that is left over is ordinary as all get-out, to the point of near invisibility. The experience isn't ordinary, but the person observing it is. Once when asked whether she was happy, the late actress Carrie Fisher answered, "Happy is one of the things I'm likely to be over the course of the day." Similarly, one of the experiences that shows up after the superego is sidelined is presence, though not necessarily most days.

Presence is boosted by the same sense of pausing in my tracks as the kind that can be willed to thwart the superego. If I feel a superego conflict in the works, I can pause and say, "Hold on a minute. What else is here?" Pause is another word for "look around." When I'm scanning my environment, it may be with an eye for the peculiar, the desirable, the fresh, the familiar, or the useful, but ultimately, I'm in the thrall of the fascinating. Looking around is being fascinated. Curiosity is the act of pulling something in my environment closer for inspection. If I want something, that means I'm curious about it; "want" and "curious" describe the same action of pulling something close. I think I want something to fulfill a need. But that's not true. I have only four needs: food, shelter, clothing, and safety. Everything else is unnecessary. What if I want things just out of the curiosity of inspecting them? That would make my superego mad; it wants me to feel that I need superfluous things, and it wants to narrow my choices to the most productive for society, or at least those that will support my structured identities. Being curious willy-nilly? That would kill the superego's right to narrow my choices.

Encountering presence is a little trippy. It can resemble a bliss state. The message that things aren't necessarily as they appear comes through. Most people who experience it want to experience it again, and again. It's typical to embark on a quest to prolong the experience. Typical, yes, but also futile. If presence is a goal, it gets gobbled up by the superego as just another way to be disappointed by what's going on right now. Paradoxically, setting a spiritual goal tends to prevent its attainment. The masterpiece on the subject is *Cutting Through Spiritual Materialism* by Chögyam Trungpa*.

Fortunately, our inner-critic work sidesteps the problem. Once the objects of the ego are identified and pushed aside, presence has a funny

---

*Trungpa's *Cutting Through Spiritual Materialism* (Boston: Shambhala Publications 1973) is not just about the ego's insidious way of taking ownership of even our most precious desires, but also presents the reader with a brilliantly clear primer on Tibetan Buddhist thought, principles, and methods.

way of showing up and taking care of itself.

Let's look a little closer at this. Goals by nature imply that things are imperfect here and now. Anytime I'm trying to find something better, I'm projecting myself out of the current moment and into the future. Most people spend a lot of time every day projecting themselves into a better future, and not noticing that satisfaction is already available. Once I've decided my current status is not quite enough, I am telling myself that I am not happy now, that there is something wrong, incomplete, or improvable in the present. Dissatisfaction is a sure hallmark of the super-ego's corrupt influence. If I'm dissatisfied by familiar life and want a trippy bliss state, then I'm in the superego's wheelhouse. Spiritualism turns into its own materialistic, attached desire for a permanent better state that is off in the distance, no different from the materialist's dream of a better world with that boat or vacation home or luxury car.

Fortunately, you don't need a spiritual goal. This process isn't simple, but it's easy. Just accept where you are and pay attention to anything that's getting in the way of your satisfaction with the current moment. As the superego – the main thing in the way – is relaxed over time, presence starts to show up, all on its own. They're two sides of the same coin: Reduce superego, increase presence. You don't need a guide to presence; you just need the kinds of exercises in this book or even, eventually, the simple acknowledgment that the parasite is here, now. If I'm aware of the superego, then I also recognize a me who deserves to pause things for a bit. And without thinking about it, I let the pause begin.

This isn't how we're taught that things work. We're told to apply ourselves to betterment, perfection, achievement of goals, disciplined behavior. Apply yourself to presence, kid. Just meditate a little more, a little harder. Sorry, but that's an unlikely path to presence. What if instead all I have to do is remark, "Hunh, that fool superego's here again." If I've done it enough times, there will suddenly appear, on occasion, space for more to enter. More is the same as presence, so long as it's more right here, right now. If I've paused to look around my most ordinary life as it is happening, in a single moment I can be introduced to the new sensations and experiences of presence. By relaxing my need to be special, to be structured, to be an achiever, a wider and less-structured world appears in living color. All on its own. You don't need to be at the top of a mountain overlooking a beautiful panorama to be soaked in awe. It can happen in the grocery line, or your office, or walking the dog. This is a process of clearing, not building. Here's Trungpa: "[I]t is not a matter of building up the awakened state of mind, but rather of burning out the confusions which obstruct it. In the process of burning out these confusions, we discover enlightenment." When I was younger, I mocked Ronald Reagan for saying his favorite occupation was clearing brush on his ranch. It proved that he was not intellectually up to the job of president. Now that I'm older, I get it. Superego work is like that. It's about clearing brush, not building fences.

TWELVE

I SEE YOU, SUPEREGO

Neshant and I had been working weekly for nine months when she said, out of the blue, "You know, I still can't believe how much things have changed for me since those first few superego encounters." It had been six months at least since Neshant had talked with her superego during our sessions. We had moved on to other exercises that I will describe in a bit.

"I feel calmer," Neshant said, "Every day. I just wanted you to know that."

Yes, I'm patting myself on the back. It's comforting to hear someone express gratitude for my expertise. That's not the main reason I'm quoting Neshant. I want you to notice that her gratitude isn't for our nine months of work – thirty or more interactions. It's for the "first few superego encounters."

Just knowing that you have a superego, that it pretends to be a real person, and that it can be addressed directly, is enough for transformation, at least for some people. It's mind-blowing. The common refrain from clients being introduced for the first time to their superego is, "I always thought that was *me*." Some add, "Why didn't I know about this before?" The dumbfounding truth is that it has been hidden in plain sight. For all of us.

Your superego badgers you from the outside, not the inside. It's a fake person who sounds like a parent. It's not very smart or complicated. It is conservative and a fearmonger. It runs your life, and it has no business doing so.

Once their nasty little parasite is known to my clients, I give them only one piece of homework, and it never changes. The rest of their lives, they carry this homework with them. I carry it with me to this day. It's this: Try to notice when your superego is active, and when you hear its voice whispering a belittling message, say these words to yourself: "That's you, superego." Simply by differentiating your superego from your core self, you win. If the messaging from the voice near your head is particularly nasty, silently say to it, "I see what you're doing. I don't deserve that." That's all you need to do. Over time, doing just that, you'll reduce the influence of your superego: "That's you, superego. I see what you're doing. I don't deserve that."

You will come to recognize its favorite playgrounds. If you notice that you feel defensive, or are in conflict with someone, or feel victimized or emotionally wrought, your superego is nearby. As soon as you are out of the trance of the conflict, see if you can find the statement, "That's you, superego." You can't necessarily stop your superego from disrupting your life – from triggering you – but you can notice afterward that it wasn't actually so helpful. You've busted it. Now it has a little less force for the next time.

After a few encounters, my clients make a game of it. They'll talk to me about their latest suffering – the boss who can't be satisfied, the inconsiderate partner, the ungrateful child – and suddenly stop and say, "Oh, that's my superego, isn't it?"

Busted.

It turns out that your superego is also the wheelhouse for all your defenses. Every potential hurt feeling is stored and cataloged by your superego, which happily brings it up to sight whenever it can. This goes beyond snarkiness into rank cruelty. Your superego wants your feelings to be fragile and wants you to be defensive. It wants you to stomp your feet, sulk, and sneer. It wants you to feel attacked and not notice that your so-called assailant is just as defensive as you are. You've bought into the idea that you're little, the world and its human manipulators are big, and you need to claw your way to the top. The superego never wants you satisfied or happy as is, because then you won't fulfill your social duty to fight your way up the pecking order.

In fact, most of your natural freedom is blocked by your superego. By putting you on defense, your snarky parasite exaggerates the risk of being your unfettered self, being creative with whatever is happening, being open to new possibilities, and it blocks you from your most outrageously alive, silly, joyful, loving, satisfied, rich, or fulfilled self.

My client Jake has been interviewing his superego, a blob with a face, for several months. "As I've gotten to know Blob," he tells me, "His influence on me has petered out. I've found that I can be more open to people, and I don't care as much about what they think of me."

So not only is life without as much superego interference *possible* – it's also desirable and, for my clients at least, preferable.

"My mind feels quieter," Jake says. "And I'm a lot less worried."

Have you encountered your superego yet?

One more thing. Don't be surprised by how it appears to you. While their ideas and talking points are all the same, superegos can appear in a multitude of guises. Mine is a classic gremlin. I've had only one client who also found hers a gremlin. Here's a partial list of my clients' superego appearances: Soccer Ball, Bigfoot, Dadig (grandmother in Armenian), Worm, Green Little Man, Betty the Artichoke, Tabby, The Face, Glenda the Good Witch, Henry, Self, Little Me, Skull, Hyena, Witch, Mom, Red Velvet Box, Librarian, Orange Ball, Red Blob, Squirrel, Thin Me, Apple, Cactus, Mom, Blue Dog, Genie, Wall, Booger, Red Balloon. All of them have an expressive face, and all of them talk.

THIRTEEN

REPEATING QUESTIONS

The material that the superego confounds, as I said, is the material of conflict. The superego creates, exaggerates, and intervenes in every conflict of my life, except the id's relatively rare survival and libido concerns. Those latter are instinctual, and the survival part at least doesn't generally involve the superego, which came along a little later in life and offers only learned responses. (I'm not getting into libido here.)

If I'm in conflict, it's a safe bet that the superego is nearby.

As we have seen, I can directly address the superego about any of its interventions and use our dialogue to get it to relax its supervision. But through another set of practical tools, I can encounter the superego indirectly and, over time, release it from a larger emotional issue that shows up for me repeatedly.

We all have our emotional pet peeves, our recurring disasters, our repetitive head-banging, our bête noirs, our blind spots, our entangled relationships. Everybody's insecure about something, and most people have a litany of insecurities. For every belief of how things should be, we're likely to have an issue with how they actually are. We have mom beliefs and issues, dad beliefs and issues, God beliefs and issues, and beliefs and issues about our competence, our perseverance, our happiness, our friendliness, our safety, our health, our looks, our athleticism, our survival skills, our worth, our ability to be loved and love, our intelligence, our openness, our spirituality, our prominence, our sexuality, our curiosity, our wealth, our status at work, our status at home, our parental capacities, our power, our value, and on and on.

These are not small things, none of them. But our superego can take any or all of them, blow them up to monstrous size and pin us to a wall of vulnerability where we're exposed and endangered and helpless and hopeless. Of course, it's wrong of the superego to do this, but before we can stop it, we have to be able to see it in action. And that's not easy. The superego is a vampire and keeps subvocal and under wraps as it wreaks its havoc. I might not even have a clue what it's messaging to me on any one insecurity. Without knowing what it's saying, how can I ask it to stop saying that? Fortunately, there's a way to trick your superego into revealing its underlying messages on any topic you choose. And you get to do it in real time, while that insecurity is raising itself. It's a method I learned from a spiritual institute in Berkeley, California, called the Ridhwan School, founded by the aforementioned A.H Almaas. It's a simple tool called "repeating questions."

I'll first show you how I use it with my clients, and then I'll explain how you can do it on your own with a friend.

Monica has been working on her superego with me for a couple of months. Thursdays at 4:00 p.m. she calls me on Skype. I ask her the same question every week: "Tell me about Monica."

She meanders around the week, what's been happening, and in a minute or two settles – as we all do if asked sincerely how things are going – on the one thing that has been bothering her in the most discouraging way lately.

On this particular Thursday, Monica's opening monologue evolves into this: "I just don't know what to make of my new boss. She's like a robot. No emotions. She goes around the table and gets updates and just nods and asks pointed questions. I know it's not just me, but it feels like she's looking right through me, or like she's impatient to get to the next person, maybe the more important person? I don't know. I feel like I don't know what to do, like she's testing me, maybe. And then I think I'll get fired, which I know is ridiculous. I'm really good at my job. They can't fire me. But why do I have to prove it to my new boss? I didn't mention, she has already picked a favorite. It's like I don't exist."

She has paused, and I interrupt and ask whether we might engage in a little exercise. It's now my job to formulate, on the fly, a series of three questions that will evoke the superego's messaging. I often take my cue from the client's last words before a pregnant pause, in this case Monica's comment before I interrupted: "It's like I don't exist."

My first question to Monica is: "Tell me a way you aren't seen."

Her instructions are to answer with the first thing that comes to mind, even if irrelevant. If nothing comes up, she can say, "I don't know." If the question bothers her, she can let me know. I will still ask it again. She can answer in the present or as if I asked about her past, in this case how she "wasn't seen." No matter what her answer, I ask the exact same question again.

"Tell me a way you aren't seen."

"I'm invisible."

"Tell me a way you aren't seen."

"My mother didn't understand me."

"Tell me a way you aren't seen."

"My boss passes right over me."

"Tell me a way you aren't seen."

"I'm Black."

"Tell me a way you aren't seen."

"Black people are invisible to white people."

"Tell me a way you aren't seen."

"No one knows the true me."

"Tell me a way you aren't seen."

"My husband doesn't take my ideas seriously."

"Tell me a way you aren't seen."

"I shrink at parties and hide myself."

This goes on for five minutes. I use a timer. If the client complains that she has run out of answers, I let her know that she can repeat old answers. At the end of five minutes, it's time for Question Two.

"What's right about feeling unseen?"

"Nothing's right about it."

"What's right about feeling unseen?"

"Nothing's right about feeling unseen."

If this answer persists, I explain that by "right" I mean useful. The superego has a reason to complain to Monica that she isn't being seen. What's "right" here doesn't mean ethically or emotionally right, but instead we're seeking what the motivation is for the superego to exaggerate the notion that Monica is unseen. "What's right about feeling unseen?"

"It feels normal."

"What's right about feeling unseen?"

"Then I might fight to be seen."

"What's right about feeling unseen?"

"It's what my mother preferred for me."

"What's right about feeling unseen?"

"I won't embarrass myself."

"What's right about feeling unseen?"

"No one will make fun of me."

"What's right about feeling unseen?"

"I'm not one of the popular girls."

"What's right about feeling unseen?"

"There's nothing right about feeling unseen."

"What's right about feeling unseen?"

"It's what people expect of me now."

After five minutes, I present the third question. I introduce it to

Monica with these words, "Now the third question is a little different. I'm going to ask you a 'feeling' question. By feeling, I mean bodily sensations, not emotional ideas. You'll answer how you answered the other two questions, but every once in a while, notice that it's a 'feeling' question, and sense into your body and describe what might be happening there as you answer the question.

"Monica, how would it feel if it was always safe to be unseen?"

"I don't know."

"How would it feel if it was always safe to be unseen?"

"I guess it would feel safe."

"How would it feel if it was always safe to be unseen?"

"It would feel lighter."

"How would it feel if it was always safe to be unseen?"

"It might feel like relief."

"How would it feel if it was always safe to be unseen?"

"I guess it would feel free, like I was flying or something."

Etcetera.

The first question gets the issue out in the open. Monica had been triggered by her boss, but like most emotional complaints, the incident doesn't stand alone. Answering the first repeating question, Monica linked her run-in with her boss with similar feelings from her childhood, produced by her mother, and with feelings of diminishment for being Black, with social phobia around friends, and with spousal conflicts. "Not being seen" is a worry that most of us have, and it has dogged Monica throughout her life. The first question gives Monica a sense of the scale and longevity of her concern over the complaint.

The second question is the most important. Having helped Monica recognize the breadth of the subject, I trick the superego into revealing its underlying, belittling messages that serve as the hidden foundation for her suffering. By asking "what's right" about the suffering, the superego is forced to reveal its reasoning. Usually, the definition of "what's right" amounts to "You've always done it," or "It's what people expect," or "It's safer." Often the reasoning is circular: "I feel unseen because I don't want to be embarrassed." Hunh? So, I resent the behavior that I encourage?

Hearing the reasoning of the superego is often humbling. The superego is not sophisticated. It's crude and it prods us as if we're still seven-year-olds.

"I've been listening to that?" Monica asks after the repeating questions. "'I'm not one of the popular girls?' Really? That's how it keeps me feeling insecure? I might as well be a first grader."

The more a client hears the reasoning of the superego, the less they take seriously the messaging.

The third question serves two purposes. First and foremost, it clues the client in to what it will feel like for her to live without that issue, that worry, that insecurity. It reminds the client that there will be a reward – actually a series of cumulative rewards – for engaging the superego in this work. Second, it gets the client to see that the feeling is already present and accessible, and that the superego is preventing her from reveling in her delighted, relaxed, relieved, free core self. Note that I'm not encouraging the client to try to feel that way in the future. This isn't a path of positive thinking, magical thinking, visualization, affirmations, agreements, or laws of attraction. Those kinds of paths have their own rules and conditions. Instead, I encourage my clients to stay in the muck for most of every session with me. I point out from time to time that my job is to torture them by asking them to describe and interrogate their suffering, over and over. I get no pleasure from this, except knowing that this vexing work seems to encourage people to break free. And for some non-masochistic reason, they return week after week.

I always construct the three repeating questions the same way: The first ("Tell me a way ...") disgorges examples of the issue at hand, tracing it through different times and circumstances. The second ("What's right about ...") tricks the superego into revealing its hidden reasoning. The third ("What would it feel like if ...) lets the client know what it will be like when that insecurity is removed. You might try it yourself with a friend.

That's at the beginning of the session. For the end of a session, I often employ a completely different technique. This one I also borrowed from the Ridhwan School, but I employ it more mechanically than the school does. I have written a book about it, *Shapes of Truth: Discover God Inside You*. A complete description of it would be a major digression here, so I will just sketch it out.

I ask my client to think about an issue that cropped up earlier that day. It can be large or small, but at the time it felt like an emotional conflict. I don't need to know what it is. Once she has signaled that she has one in mind, I tell her to forget about it for now. I ask her to sit up straight, take a couple of breaths, and close her eyes. Then I ask her to do something most people have never done before. I ask her to scan inside her torso, her neck, and her head, looking for a localized feeling. I say it might be a feeling of tension or constriction, or a tremble, or a hot spot or cold spot, just something that subtly sticks out but isn't obviously a gastrointestinal issue.

After a bit, she'll say, "I've got one."

I then ask a series of questions, in this order:

"Where is it located?"

"How tall is it?"

"How wide is it?"

"How thick is it?"

"Is it more toward the front, middle or back of your body?"

"Does it have a shape?"

"Are its corners sharp or rounded?"

"What's its density?"

"What do you think it's made of?"

"Does it have a skin or is it the same inside and out?"

"Is the center hollow or full?"

"Is it attached to anything or is it free-floating?"

"Is it moving or still?"

"What color is it?"

By the time she has finished, she might have described, for instance, a brown, three-inch in diameter rubber ball lodged in her solar plexus that feels tense. In fact, that's a quite typical body-form of this sort; but it could also be a cylinder across the shoulders or a band across her forehead or any number of possibilities. I then ask her to do nothing but observe it inside and out, paying attention only to its physical properties.

"Don't concern yourself with how it got there or what it means, or whether you like it or not," I tell the client. "Your only care is its physical characteristics. Describe to me anything you haven't mentioned, and then let me know if anything changes. There's no hurry. Nothing has to change. Just keep looking at it."

After a while – anywhere from less than a minute to sixty minutes, with a mean of about five – the client will notice the shape start to change. Ultimately, usually within twenty minutes, it will disappear from her body. Once it has completely disappeared, I ask her, "How do you feel now?"

The answer is almost always the same: "I feel good. I feel really good, like there's nothing wrong."

In this case, the encounter hasn't been directly with the superego, or even with its reasoning. This time the client has encountered an objectified view of the result of the superego's belittling messages: the truth of the client's *belief* in the emotional issue that is dragging her down. This brown or gray object represents everything the client believes about the issue. The issue might be Monica being unseen. The issue might be the ingratitude of a grown child. The issue might be guilt over hurting someone's feelings. Big or small, it gets taken out of the regular vocabulary of words and moved into a mysterious vocabulary of body-forms. Because the brown rubber ball is an inert visual, the client won't feel a need to fix it, run away from it, or replace it with something nicer. Because the body-form is benign and doesn't have the emotional force of her superego, she can be curious about it without resenting it. The client just looks at it. When it feels it has been looked at enough, it disappears. And inevitably, the client is left with the feeling that not only is that issue gone, but all their issues are gone – not forever, but for a short respite that feels pretty good.

These two techniques – repeating questions and body-form inquiry – not only reinforce the superego Gestalt that we started with, but eventually they become the focus of the work. The client doesn't need to engage the superego directly anymore to recognize that the parasite is at work, and by identifying it move away from its influence.

"I always think I'm doing the repeating questions wrong, or they're too hard," Monica says. "But somehow, they always leave me thankful that I have learned something about myself. Something useful. And then the body work, wow, does that take me to some weird places. But I can't explain it, I just feel all right, sometimes for a few days afterward. It's quite mysterious even though it happens every time."

FOURTEEN

IDENTIFY YOUR DEFENSES

T he superego hungers for you to be defensive. It keeps you on guard, exaggerating dangers both real and imagined. If the danger is real – sometimes a hostile boss is a hostile boss – then the superego persuades you to defend yourself, actively, every chance you have. The more helpful advice would be to do what the job requires and address the hostility only when necessary. And not to obsess about it. A friend, for instance, would tell us to look at the situation clearly, figure it out, and settle on a strategy if necessary. Then fit it into your workday as appropriate. But that's not the superego's *modus operandi*. The superego belittles, harangues, and talks to you about everything except the actual strategy. And the superego always wins. How can you retain objectivity when your superego is muttering that you're about to be fired, and reminding you in the background that you're defective and an impostor?

Part of grappling with your superego is recognizing your own defensiveness. Your defensiveness is both created and managed by the superego. There seems to be no way out of it. Everybody complains about the inner critic. Hardly anyone does anything about it. The superego tells me I'm small, which strands me in the belief that I have to defend myself from someone bigger.

Let's explore this counterproductive behavior of the superego. Let's look at its tricks and tools.

What are its defenses? I'm going to make this simple. First, we have to dismiss the *id* defenses. For the survival instinct, the defensive attitudes are fight or flight. For the libido instinct, they're sublimation or sexual aggression. When we're dealing with the superego, we're not involved in those defenses.

The superego defenses boil down to three: withdrawal, anger, and self-righteousness. That's right. You have only three defenses*. You can get sad and sulk, you can get mad, or you can scorn. It's funny to think about that. We all believe that we're a wild network of possible defenses, that we have a grab bag of stored clever responses, and that we can create new ones on the fly. But we're much simpler than that. Our grab bag has exactly three shopworn items to choose from: withdrawal, anger, or self-righteousness.

Worse yet, we have only three issues that we're constantly defending ourselves against. Each of the three defenses responds to its own issue. The issue of not being seen results in withdrawal. The issue of not being in control results in anger. The issue of not being seen as right results in self-righteousness. One of the three is dominant for you; you tend to see that danger more than the other two and defend yourself with its instrument. Academic psychologists give a fancy, horribly pejorative name to

---

*The three defenses were shown to me in the writings and talks of Hameed Ali, a teacher and prolific writer whose pen name is A.H. Almaas. His brilliant psychospiritual take on the development of the ego and its defensive mechanisms is *The Pearl Beyond Price: Integration of Personality into Being: An Object Relations Approach* (Boston: Shambhala Publications 1988). Some of the other ideas and exercises herein also were introduced to me by Ali and his books. For more than five years I regularly attended retreats and inquiry-laden weekends led by Ali and others he has trained in his Diamond Approach curriculum. We did a lot of repeating questions. If I were still one to carry debts, I would owe my own pearl beyond price to Ali.

your diagnosis. If you tend to withdraw, you have *schizoid* personality traits. If you tend to anger, you have *borderline* personality traits. If you tend to be self-righteous, you have *narcissistic* personality traits. Ugh. The labels of damning. Academic psychologists can show their medical bias, naming the defenses as if they are always pathological responses that need to be cured. That may be true in some cases, but there's something weird about calling something that everybody has a disease. It's like calling my brain a disease. Some brains are diseased, but most are not.

None of the three defenses is wrong to have, and none is worse than the others. The fact is that you need to defend yourself sometimes to get what you want. In a society of distrust, your only defenses are to walk away, show some aggression, or call out the falsity of the other person's position. (As with the id, freezing isn't a real defense. It's an unpleasant failure to present a defense.) You might ask, what about the response of forgiveness or tolerance? We're talking only about the times that you notice yourself being defensive. Most of us believe that we're first tolerant and accepting, and then Plan B is to get defensive. This viewpoint is unpleasant to us, but obviously necessary. It's impossible to imagine a civilized, industrialized society, a place where trust constantly needs to be managed, without some conflicts that would naturally lead to defensive behaviors. These human defenses are the three weaponized shields that we all are provided with. No one has a fourth; the three are useful enough to handle any situation. At some point in your life you've withdrawn from someone, you've gotten angry at someone, and you've mocked someone.

As I said, one of the three defenses is dominant in each of us. This is the work of the superego. The superego decided when you were about seven which defense would be your default. One of your parents is usually the model for that defense. If your father was controlling, he probably exhibited anger. Anger is always frustration over lack of control. You might have taken his model and adopted it, in which case you would likewise default to anger when under pressure. Or you might have rejected him, felt as if you were misunderstood by him, and chosen withdrawal as your defense. If your mother told you to be demure and quiet in order to be accepted, your superego likewise might have chosen withdrawal, or you might have rebelled, with your superego steering you to be a talkative know-it-all. Whichever of the three defenses was selected as your default, your superego amplified it and kept it alive, and you still have it. It would be quite unusual to change your default defense anytime in your life. The other two defenses are certainly available to you, but you generally try them only when your default doesn't get the reaction you expect.

I'll describe them a little more so you can find your own default, your strong second, and your weak third.

Being Seen

If you're a woman or a person of color, you may know this one intuitively, socially. But at a more fundamental level, everyone feels the childhood wound of not being seen for our true selves. The whole reward system concentrates on our external behaviors rather than our inner beauty. At some point as a child, you noticed that you were a puppet of your parents' wishes for you. You might have been trotted out to play the violin for guests. Or you got the biggest cheers from your parents when they were on the sports sidelines. Or the opposite: You were shamed for bad grades or bad manners. In any of these scenarios, a piece of you cried out, "This isn't the real me. This is for show. You don't know the real me." How often are kids over three rewarded for just being the goofballs, daydreamers, and lovebugs that they are? Rarely. We're all tragically reminded that our perfect inborn value isn't enough, isn't worth knowing, and when the lesson is case-hardened that no one really cares about that part of us, we give up on being known for our beautiful souls. And we resent it.

The defense of being misunderstood – withdrawal – seems weirdly self-defeating. "You don't know the real me? Well, I won't show you *any* me." As the defender collects herself in another room, she might notice that now she is even less seen, and also lonely. Another way of looking at it is as the "You can't fire me. I quit!" defense. By exiting the misunderstanding, I'm no longer misunderstood. If this is you, conflict might lead you to clam up, sulk, head into another room, feel wounded, refuse eye contact, feel a collapse as if moving inward, cover your ears, or dive under the covers. You might leave and take a walk. You might call a friend and make an immediate date. You might pick up a device and start scrolling mindlessly. Healthy or unhealthy, these are all defensive strategies. You've been triggered, and you responded in your withdrawal way.

Being In Control

When we're little, parents are giants, physically and metaphorically. They are huge and lurking as they peer down at us. They could snap us like twigs. They control our movements and even, to an extent, our thoughts. They command. "Look at me, young lady." They control. "Go to your room and come out when you can be nicer to your brother." They control what we eat, when we sleep, what toys are present, and whether we can visit with friends. We're at their mercy, and their beck and call. We're as imprisoned in their control as a pet dog. Regrettably, though, we seem to be born with a knack for exploring and willy-nilly curiosity. Then parents get in the way of our freedom to explore. This creates conflict. Temper tantrums, mostly.

The defense of anger – it always represents frustration over lack of control – gets a bad rap. Because it can escalate into physical violence, the culture tends to fear anger more than withdrawal or self-righteousness. But in its normal guise, it's safe and equal in dramatic effect and persuasiveness to the other two. It has the same weight. Psychologists point out that defenses aren't dangerous until they cross an imaginary line into "acting out." Unfortunately, there's no agreed-on point at which appropriate countermeasures devolve into "acting out." You know that you're trying to take back control if you're shouting, stomping your feet, find your face going red, feel a chest-expanding rising bile, heading toward name-calling, or trying to jump out of your own skin. Don't worry so much about it. It's just the default defense you're stuck with, no matter what others think. I'm now going to lapse into gender stereotypes: It's more acceptable in males, which is why they seem to get over anger quicker than women, who are prone to have it prolonged by feelings of remorse and guilt over *losing* control – perhaps the super-ego-subscribed fear from childhood that an angry woman will be exiled or shunned, or divorced, or locked into the witch stocks.

Being Right

Parents are encouraged to praise precocious behavior. They worry when baby Eduardo is late to crawling or, God forbid, isn't learning words fast enough. They look hopefully for signs that they bore a rare child prodigy. But there are two sides to being precocious. The obvious one is that the child is smart and resourceful, capable, and seemingly born to lead in something. The hidden side is that the child believes that success is up to them, and the world might not be supportive. The precocious child tends to evolve into the insecure, narcissistic adult, the know-it-all who scorns the value of others and fears for his or her own lovability.

Narcissism sounds terrible, doesn't it? It gets confused with narcissistic personality disorder, which *is* a terrible affliction. But we're all narcissists to some extent; it just means that in seeing the world through our own eyes, we develop the habit of believing our own interpretations of what we see. Each of the defenses has a sociopathic extreme – the all-out withdrawal of the hermit, the radical anger of the sadist, and the radical self-righteousness of the malignant narcissist or zealot. Most of you don't have to worry about that. Hardly anyone gets the sociopathic version. If you default to everyday narcissism, you're the harmless dinner guest who is heavy on sarcasm, dismissive of other people's ideas, and impatient to speak. You might talk over people and finish their sentences, correct your spouse's grammar, and say "Really?" from time to time. (My wife snarls at me when I use the interrogative "Really?" as a complete sentence.) You wonder why people would be offended. You're just offering up good counsel and a trove of memorized knowledge. In an emotional pickle, your defense is passive aggression. Contempt wipes out your adversary.

That's it. Those are the only three social defenses, and one of them is your strong suit. With its alarmist trickery, the superego can raise your default defense time after time, without your ever noticing your tacit approval. Knowing that might sound discouraging – who wants to be stuck in a continuous tape loop? – but it's quite the opposite. By recognizing your default, you can get yourself out of a conflict faster and more completely.

Conflict exists. We can't expect to get through a day without someone or something thwarting our plans or desires. We're just too busy and interconnected an ant farm for my needs and desires not to run afoul of a fellow ant's. Your responsibility here isn't to avoid all conflict, or even to remove all your reactivity. As Ram Dass said: After decades of spiritual work, he didn't lose a single neurosis. But his *attitude* toward his neuroses changed. He could shrug with humor when he caught himself in an old defense. In Mickey Lemle's 1992 documentary *Compassion in Exile*, the Dalai Lama laughs that his advance team – the specialists who are committed to the details of his appearances – probably see him as short-tempered. He doesn't disagree; he just knows to recognize it and take it lightly enough that it can correct itself. Sounds paradoxical, right? But Ram Dass and the Dalai Lama know that they are human and will at times be frustrated by their lack of control over events. You and I, too, will be frustrated, annoyed, and flabbergasted at the obstacles, misunderstandings, and outright sabotage in the way of our best-laid plans. What do we do?

We wait. We wait until our first reaction has burnt itself out. We might notice that we're sulking, or flashing temper, or sarcastically dismissing someone. In the heat of the moment, we're not going to stop it. But as soon as there's a pause in the action, our responsibility is to switch gears and ask, "Which of the defenses am I using? Is my issue being seen, being in control, or being right?" And then ask, "Which of the defenses is my antagonist using? Does her issue look like sulking, anger, or self-righteousness?" By asking these questions, you've removed yourself from the trivial fight that has been engaged, and you're seeing the pattern of your life, and if the conflict is with a close friend or partner, the dancelike repetition of your give-and-take. By abstracting your view into a bird's-eye pattern, you can better notice how ridiculously exaggerated you have made the danger of not getting what you want.

My wife and I met late in life, so we're blessedly free of many arguments. Fights are just too tiring for worn-out old people, who find it easier to give in with a shrug. But occasionally a nerve gets hit, and the two of us are off and running like youngsters. Annie's default is withdrawal, and mine is self-righteousness. That's oil and water. As she leaves the room, I'm following after her letting her know how right I am and how wrong she must therefore be. Actually, it never gets quite that physical. Maybe it will, when we're in the old folks' bin, reduced to only one TV remote. Mostly she finds herself sulking and licking her wounds in the bedroom, while I'm left indignant, standing in the kitchen, and muttering to myself. Then, poof, I remember that I have this weird app that demands that I be right, and that Annie has her own app that demands that she be understood. At around this point, I remember hearing her say from time to time, "Would you rather be right or happy?" And though the correct answer is "both," I get the point. Wait, I think, she needs to be seen and understood. Why don't I help this along by having that happen? And that encourages me to start asking her open-ended questions, like, "Maybe I didn't get this entirely right. Why don't you tell me what you need and how I'm interfering with it?" We start in again, but this time talking like friends who are trying to resolve a situation. Okay, maybe not immediately, but eventually counts, too. She may not get what she wants, but she'll be heard. I may not get what I want, but my opinion will be respected.

I have three other little tools that help me separate from my defensive self-righteousness. Tool One is to blame myself for every conflict that I'm in. This is not as stupid as it might seem. Saying the words, "I am 100 percent responsible for this conflict" has a way of stopping my zealotry in its tracks. The fly in the ointment is that I have to believe it even if my antagonist hasn't signed on to this system. In fact, she may likewise believe that I am 100 percent responsible for the conflict. Still, I know it's pretty true that my annoyance is my own business, not hers. And that's because of my second tool.

I call Tool Two the "Ninety-nine Others" consideration. Here's an example. It happens that my wife dislikes farce, even if it's brilliantly written by Oscar Wilde or Michael Frayn. When it's my turn to pick the movie and I insist on farce, I can anticipate a sullen death mask being positioned a couple of feet to my left on the couch, its life-sapping energy pulling at me peripherally minute after minute until I give up and hand the remote to her. It's not that my wife lacks a sense of humor; we spend large portions of the day inside sketch comedies that she spontaneously invents. She just doesn't have time for witty, sarcastic, and pointed British takedowns. Time after time I have felt defeated as I tried to share my sophisticated taste for snark with her. And each time I've been left muttering to myself. And then I remember the Ninety-nine Others gimmick. Here's how it works: I mentally line up ninety-nine people in a row, starting to my immediate right and standing shoulder to shoulder, male and female, all adults, heading off neatly to the horizon. I recognize that not a single one of them is at all bothered by what I consider my wife's deficient consideration for my aesthetic. I can take anything annoying about anyone and find ninety-nine people to line up and shrug, "What's the big deal?" If the trait is annoying enough, I might have to search through an imaginary billion or so people to find ninety-nine who aren't bothered, but I know they're out there in the world. If what irritates me doesn't bother them, then it's probably my own damn fault that it makes me defensive.

Which brings me to Tool Three. Once I have moved this far away from the original conflict, I can remember the simple truth that *no one* is on offense. No one attacks. Everyone is on defense. My wife isn't attacking me with her sullen withdrawal. She isn't shutting me up to win. She is moving away from me to protect her own turf, her own needs, her own insecurities. *Everyone* is always on the defensive. This is weird but true. It's even true in geopolitics. No one ever admits to firing the first shot, and if the videotape proves that one side did, they'll always say, truthfully, that it was "preemptive." They were defending against a future injury by attacking.

Here are the three tools in summation:

It's all my fault.

Ninety-nine people wouldn't be annoyed. At all.

No one is attacking me. Everyone is on defense.

You're going to be defensive. You can't stop cringe from happening. But you can stop it from sticking around, and over time you can free yourself from most of your insecurity. It doesn't matter if you get triggered. It only matters that you don't let the moment prolong itself into a sullen, or angry, or self-righteous mood. All conflict is pretty simple: Your professed need and your antagonist's professed need can't share the same space. You're given a choice. You think it's win, lose, or draw. But it's simpler than that. You are facing your temporary adversary's request for his or her need to be fulfilled. That's all that is going on. You have three possible responses: Yes, no, or compromise. What's the big emotional deal about yes, no, or compromise?

FIFTEEN

WASTE YOUR TIME

My clients complain they're overwhelmed. They feel the civilized pressures of numerous expectations – to advance at work, to launch their children well, to improve their marriages, to get healthy, to save the world from global warming, to find purpose after retirement. They are concerned about something they call "wasting time."

What is it to waste time? Is time really a resource that needs to be replenished like money? If I'm not doing time right, then am I lazy? Procrastinating? Distracting myself? Pandering to whim? Being sinful? Self-indulgent? So many descriptions are available to belittle me for not *spending* my time *fruitfully*.

God help us if we were put on this earth to achieve, lead, and maintain constant productivity. These are the concerns of social maintenance. For me to spend all my time in protection of my species seems weirdly biological, as if the Darwinian explanations – getting the species firmly lodged in every niche possible – were all that we had. As if puttering in the garden were worthless. The longer I live, the more I'm convinced that my only so-called purpose is to be fascinated – by my garden, my friends, my children, my partner, politics, my work, my play, my own self, and whatever else I am dragged into doing. So how do I resolve such a notion with my culturally cultivated sense that productivity defines me, gives me purpose, and provides me with a moral grounding for my decisions? All of which is true to my social self, right?

For decades I was, like my clients, scared of my own tendency to procrastinate. Why did I put off things that I knew had to be completed? I woke to a sink full of dishes. My desk drawer contained two quarter-finished novels. My annual strategy plan was due tomorrow; time to cram. I stared at a shelf of well-intended, unopened boxes of thank-you cards. Who was stopping me from completing these simple tasks and challenging projects? Why did the undone lists repeat themselves daily to me, reminding me of my own stack of to-dos that weren't getting done? I assumed that I was a procrastinator, and, if so, not a very mature, responsible person after all.

We've entered the nerve center of the superego.

If my job is to always be productive, then my failure is procrastination and laziness. I shouldn't notice that everything gets done, that when I'm supposedly procrastinating, I'm actually just choosing to do other things, usually smaller, less frightening tasks. When do I stall out on a project? Mostly when I've hit a roadblock – often a surprising variable that I know little about. Do I immediately call for help? No, I delay instead, thinking it's up to me to figure it out. In the meantime, I manage the rest of my life, somehow. The other time I collapse and put off the next step is when I idealized the result. As I approach the end of the project, it becomes clear that my model – the Great American Novel if I'm a writer, the viral app if I'm a programmer – is beyond reach. I don't recognize that the novel I've written, the app I've designed is good enough for government work and deserves to be completed. The Tao Te Ching has a relevant line: Most failure happens on the verge of success. So, am I lazy or am I being browbeaten by a superego that expects me to know things I don't and to perfect things I can't?

What's the solution? How about this? I don't expect too much of myself, and by the end of a project, I am focused on completing it for no other reason than to be free to do something else. That kind of attitude might be worth trying on.

By the time I'm three-quarters through a project, the quality is already baked in. If there's a market for the thing I've created – say this book – by then I have either met the market's expectations or I probably never will, no matter how much I edit and change and "improve" what I've got mostly down on paper. We're 80 percenters, and so is our audience. It's more forgiving than we think. But we get tied up in all sorts of refining, mostly out of concern that we haven't concealed the 20 percent of ourselves that might be a little messy.

Because we're such meaning-making machines, we mistake the end of a thought, event, project, or lesson for a meaning. But the end is just the end. If you think about it, meaning and end are identical. They describe my mind reading back to me what just happened. Whatever it is, it's supposed to end there so that I'm free to do the next thing, unburdened. But most people think the end is subsumed within a consequence and that the project *isn't* finished until the world offers feedback through sales or accolades or their opposites. Hand it to the superego to always be thinking ahead. What if the consequence is just another beginning? Most writers I know have a fondness for arranging words into essays or books. And the same people are annoyed by what happens next – publishing and marketing. For me, it's kind of fun to write a book; it's misery to sell it. But the people working in the publishing house might have the opposite view. It's no fun to wait for an author to write a book; the good stuff starts when the manuscript drops on the desk. Same two extended moments; opposite responses. Neither is more meaningful, more correct, better, or worse. Orson Welles put it simply when asked what kind of emotion he wanted the moviegoer to leave with: "If you want a happy ending, that depends, of course, on where you stop your story." A lot of us don't notice that what we're worrying about ended a long time ago. We're dangerously close to the territory of the annoying friend who constantly chirps, "Lighten up." If meaning and purpose aren't all they're cracked up to be, then maybe I'm plenty productive already, and I should, God forbid, lighten up.

Two contemporary metaphors for feeling overwhelmed are "running out of bandwidth" and "multitasking." Oddly, neither of them is at all accurate. We humans always operate with the exact same amount of bandwidth and hardly any of us multitask. This is hard to believe, but my run-around days as the father of four in a demanding corporate job had just as much bandwidth as my days of writing, publishing, taking in clients, and gardening. What we call free will – our view of ourselves operating in cause and effect – operates within a single-band metaphysics that can only experience one read-back at a time. If I think I'm doing two things at once – looking at the red leaves on the tree while I navigate the crosswalk – the appropriate metaphor would be Internet packet technology. I'm doing a little crosswalk caution, then a little leaf observation, then another bit of crosswalk, another bit of leaves, and so on. One thing at a time, in a single train of thought that is exactly one experience wide – approximately the breadth of a sentence fragment – at all times. My two concerns might be more annoying: finishing a work project while on hold for the school counselor. But it's always going on one at a time. So how can I be overwhelmed? The myth of multitasking is so widespread that it might seem irrelevant to debunk it. Most researchers discredit multitasking altogether, and those who believe that some people are capable of doing two things at once (less than 3 percent of the population in one study) find that they still don't get more done.

Here comes the parasite again, raining on my parade. If my thoughts were restricted to what's happening now, and the next now, and the next, as they happened, then I wouldn't notice much burden. Most moments are quite simple and benign like that. They have a beginning of curiosity, a middle in which the variables I've chosen are combined into a new form, and an end of release and light playback. When I am not being badgered by the gremlin, I invent a puzzle for myself, solve it, and move on to the next thing. Left to their own devices, most moments seem to have their own lightness of being. All are remarkable, and none's much more meaningful than another. It feels just like play, that. But my parasite begs to differ. In its constant buzzkill of narrowing my interests to the most mundane protection of the species, the superego enters my thoughts with judgments and lists and predictions of doom. We've talked about judgments already; now let's get into lists.

We are busy creatures, humans in the 21st century. We have full calendars of people and happenings, most of them contributing to our ability to maintain our possessions, including not only material objects but also the upkeep of our family relationships, our positions, and our personal identities. We have a lot to sort out, and so we have to-do lists. Sometimes it gets so busy that I have to write down my list, and it spreads across the page, two columns and forty items, most of which are likely to come to a head within a week. That physical list is quite helpful to me. For one thing, it reminds me that I hardly need to increase my productivity, no matter what my superego might think. I'm already busy!

My mental to-do list is quite another thing. It is a nag. It enters my mind without my asking, and in the superego's usual bullying way expresses mild scorn and disdain for my ability to keep up appearances. That list – which usually introduces itself with an "uh-oh" – is oddly unhelpful. How do I know this? Because for a while I paid special attention to it and tracked it as it appeared on average a couple of dozen times a day. It might have been looping a hundred or more times – I don't know – but I caught it a couple of times an hour. As part of my dialogue with my superego, I asked for some freedom from my to-do list. Begrudgingly and with a warning that I would fail in my responsibilities, my gremlin eventually agreed to bring up the list once in the morning and once in the late afternoon. And that's when I hear the list now, and it's quite enough for me to meet my scheduled duties. I read my calendar when I get up in the morning – that's No. 1 – and check it toward the next day's schedule before bed – that's No. 2. When my superego tries to nag me in between, I say, "Thanks, but I don't need that." On the other hand, there are days when I'm forgetful, and I am able all on my own to open my smartphone calendar to double-check. I don't need a superego to remind me. My authentic self accepts my forgetfulness and isn't a nag.

A lot of worry disappears when my calendar belongs to me, not my gremlin. Even if it is full of other people's expectations for me – pressing appointments, overlapping projects – can I review my calendar without apprehension? It turns out I can trust myself to be reasonably responsible. And if I'm not so worried about the next thing and the one to follow, it's more of a delight when the new activity actually appears. That's the other thing about to-do lists: They're ranked. Built into them is a judgment that the duties on the list are worth more than anything not on the list. We all buy into this. If I had to pick one recurring activity that should stand out for me most days, as if highest ranked, it would be my walk into town. About 85 percent of what's lovely, true, and worthwhile in the universe can be found on any ten-minute walk. Does my daily walk appear on any of my to-do lists? Of course not. I was trained to "sneak in" the walk. I'm fine with that, but it's funny if I think about it. The items on my superego's to-do lists are more likely activities to be avoided: an unpleasant conversation, a challenging task, the stuff we call the grind. If I'm reminding myself repeatedly of them, they "weigh more heavily," which means they've developed their own emotional shells that join with mine. One thing I discovered as I reduced my superego's list-telling was that the formerly annoying activities lost a lot of their weight. If I was allowed to keep my own schedule, it seemed to have more time, and I was more likely to just do the next thing as it came up. As I removed the judgments and emotion from my activities, my sense of being too busy, overwhelmed, burdened, and annoyed died down. Paradoxically, I took on more challenges; they drew my curiosity and masteries but didn't seem any more taxing than the dishes or watching TV. Conversely, TV no longer presents itself as a distraction but as a perfectly fine, if mediated, activity. Time and effort are all the same to me, whether I'm working with clients, writing this book, gardening, taking a walk, or watching TV, and all of them can draw my curiosity and meaning-making apparatus equally.

I mentioned earlier that I oversee more than 300 shrubs, flowers, and trees. My preference is to putter. I'm not here to learn about gardening. I've mastered other activities, from the trombone and American literature in my teens to newspapering, corporate management, and coaching in my adulthood. Some people keep learning new subjects. Not me, not these days. Every time I try – guitar lessons with Annie, a late-life master's program in Eastern Classics – my superego gets a quick foothold and I'm back in a world of achievement, comparison, and suffering. Such a drag. Which isn't to say that I haven't learned how to garden; I just haven't tried to master it. I've allowed myself the luxury of slow and laborious trial and error, planting here and there until I amassed a large and, I suspect, complete set of flora that amuses me endlessly. I look, I catalog, I respond. I snip here and there, clear brush, weed, fertilize a little, spray my fruit trees, harvest a few pears at a time, mow the lawns, rake and blow the leaves, prune the peach tree back 30 percent, drive to the nursery for replacement plants or sod or planting soil – whatever needs to be done on that day. Whether my plants are dying in a drought or thriving in a deluge, my habits are the same. At some point most days I find myself wandering around, looking at these strange little beings that I tend. We're so curious, us humans, and what piques us is change. So, without asking to, my mind notices what's different – new dove's-foot crane's-bill weeding its way through the ferns, a wilt where yesterday stood a magnificent violet iris, peaches growing fur, Brussels sprouts now ribbing the stalk, sycamore leaves rotting into dark brown mush where caught under the geraniums.

My time is neither wasted nor fulfilled. I *experience* my garden. Simply by my being fascinated by it, my yard seems to take care of itself mostly, especially the brilliant roses who know all there is about resource preservation. By treading lightly with my own purpose as a gardener, I'm able to peer through my defenses and see the spectacle of the blossoming, fading, dying, or sleeping, re-emerging, new looks, as these simple little lives do what they do.

It's a good model for me, puttering. I putter whether writing, seeing clients, gardening, or taking a walk. It's *all* puttering. Only the scale differs. Some puttering takes a moment; other activities sort out for months. When bad thoughts appear, and they do, they're puttering, too. They amble in and amble out, occasionally collecting into moods like rose bushes fading, losing blossoms and leaves, and a few weeks later blooming again.

A word about politics. People on TV and in my circle of friends and family continually show me how to be indignant, frustrated, worried, and ashamed about how things are going. Whether I'm for or against redistributing wealth, for or against social justice, for or against the current Supreme Court or president, I'm encouraged to be hot and bothered. My superego loves this; it makes its job much easier. My parasite can run amok among all the choices for where to place my anxiety: climate change, poverty, opportunity, charity, religion, political party, war, refugees, the border, abortion, and the list goes on. I'm supposed to believe that my position on each of these political subjects matters more than my interest in my wonderful garden. I can only respond with one word: *Really?*

I vote, I occasionally march, and I watch a half hour of television news most weekdays. A couple of times a week I leaf through a few digital newspapers and magazines. Every once in a while I doomscroll through Twitter. That's about it, and I'm pretty sure that's enough, for me. *You* might be a precinct worker or a lobbyist, a policy wonk, or an activist. Then *you'll* have good reason to spend more time than me on politics. *You* have *your* job in the web of humans supporting their species; I have mine. Me, I keep my social concerns largely separate from my personal exploration of life. This is what Jesus was talking about when he told us to render unto Caesar that which is Caesar's. What he really meant was for us to *not* render unto Caesar that which *isn't* Caesar's, which is most of my life. As far as I can tell, despite what most preachers say, Jesus was thoroughly apolitical. He wasn't talking about redistribution of wealth when he said the poor in spirit have it all over the rest of us. The Good Samaritan isn't a charity story, but Jesus discovering the inborn universality of compassion. Rich people aren't screwed in Christ's view because they're rich, but because they're trapped in their accumulations. Poor people aren't better off because they have little, but because they have given up on wanting silly things. These stories have much more to do with my personal, everyday life among my close neighbors than with my ballot choices.

If I'm in the world of politics and social justice, then I'm separating the population into bullies and victims, and spending my time trying to right wrongs. To do so, I must view people through their identities, which gets in the way of my ability to empathize.

Indignation, frustration, anxiety, and shame operate when I'm separated from compassion; they frame and support my defenses. They push away other people as offenders. They can be intoxicating, buttressing our own sense of having differentiated, independent selves. They do everything except recognize how we are all the same, and common in purpose and essence. Martin Luther King Jr. said, "Hate cannot drive out hate. Only love can do that." Jesus said there's no such thing as an enemy. If you could live like that, you might find yourself closer to those near you and less concerned about people far away. That doesn't make you selfish; it means you're living a balanced life. Every day 150,000 people on this planet die. A third of those die before their time – through accidents, war, disease, starvation, homicide, neglect. Those 50,000 poor souls represent 1/150,000th of the 8 billion available souls that day. Which of them are you responsible for, every day? You'll never run out of things to frustrate or worry you if you want to focus on those 50,000 people every day. A new 50,000 shows up every day, effortlessly. And you'll never notice that the species has spread everywhere and has reached an inconceivable number, almost all of them fed, clothed, and housed, and living on average twice as long as they did for the 300,000 years before 1900. What I'm saying here isn't popular, and of course I pitch in when

I can. But I think you're supposed to have a chance to enjoy yourself
most of the time during whatever number of years you've been given. It's
not shameful to be content.

SIXTEEN

GOD AND RELIGION

Since everyone who appears to be doing well is most likely under the control of their superego, why would I want to quiet mine? Being different is not so fun. I already lived through the awkwardness of eighth grade. Do I really want to develop a new way of being an outcast in the world?

It's true that the world will change for you as your superego subsides, but not how you expect. Your everyday life won't alter much, at least from the outside. You'll have the same friends and family, job and vacations, pastimes, and music. But you probably will notice a disruption to some more private notions, especially of God and religion.

Uncomfortable as the subject may be, *spirituality* is bound to raise its hoary head when the parasite recedes to the sidelines. This may be an unintended consequence for you. You thought you were just getting rid of a pest, but in its place new, peculiar notions will appear. After doing some superego work, for instance, atheists may experience God. I did. Christians and Jews may turn Buddhist. Evangelicals may question their preachers.

Think of your superego as a set of filters. It not only narrows your choices to the most conservative, repetitive, fearful, and belittling ones possible in the everyday world. By containing you in one set of circumstances, it tends to sap the world of its colors, its wild and messy beauty. The grumbler stuck in a world of distrust sees black and white. The whistler exploring the possibilities might see a rainbow. As the black and white filter disintegrates, new and different colors pour in. The spectrum is limitless.

I experienced this in a literal fashion after having my Gestalt conversations with my gremlin. When enough filters had been shifted to the periphery, one day I had a vision of a set of velvet stage curtains parting to show first a glimpse and then a slice and eventually a panorama of shimmering light shows and special effects. The metaphor wasn't lost on me, and it helped teach me to look beyond the ordinary. Over time, the everyday physical world came to seem more vivid, its colors saturated like after a rainfall, better outlined and somehow happier. My senses were rewarded even before my belief systems started to break apart.

Partly I was just more caught up in the moment itself. The parasite wants me to be uneasy where I am and urges me to consider how much happier I could be if things were slightly different, a little better, and more productive. Under its influence I ignore the beauty right here, and skip ahead into a conceptual set of possibilities, both desirable and horrific. When the gremlin's voice quieted for me, I paused in more moments of the day, and discovered that they had natural delights worth appreciating.

It turns out that we humans, even the most dogmatically atheistic, are all religious metaphysicians. We're all curious about how *it all* works. Mostly we are stuck with trying to get it to work better. But if I could relax into the world as if it were self-supporting, then all my notions about how to live a good life would be turned upside down. For me, this less-filtered world showed such distinctly different conditions that I found myself rethinking all my well-considered arguments about God, about who I was in relation to others, what was important, and my own purpose and meaning. If there were more here when I removed my conditioning, what might the expanded view offer me?

As this wider world opens up as it did for me, you might have to deal with older preconceptions about God and religion. Like any underlying assumptions, spiritual ones need to be revealed and deconstructed through close examination.

This can be especially unsettling to your superego, who might resist such explorations, claiming that without the stability of your core beliefs about what is, you'll float into a world that lacks logic and morality. God and religion often carry the belittling weight of the superego. While it's generally not their intention, spiritual bosses – both the heavenly ones with the beards, lightning bolts, and superpowers, and the flesh-and-bone preacher/guru/imam/rabbi types –have their own way of making me cower. They may threaten me with original sin, or hell, or stoning, or ostracism, or a pledge card for a tithe I don't really want to pay. Like parents they appear often in the role of superior authorities. And as their inferior, I am reduced to a seven-year-old. Ever been guilt-tripped? Don't you shrink in your own estimation?

All institutions, including religious ones, have a component of social restraint, limiting your possibilities. They're all like high school with its hall passes and assigned seats, and an authority figure up front telling you what to do. We join clubs, religions, schools, and Facebook groups with an intention to improve ourselves. At least that's what we think. Mostly we're establishing a tribal identity. I'm in the Baptist tribe. I'm in the Grateful Dead tribe. I'm in the gardening tribe. I'm in the social worker tribe. As civilized adults living among strangers, we're desperate for a safe tribe where for a bit of our lives we can default to trust. By agreeing to the same values as the other club members, I can safely predict the future within their midst. That's not necessarily so in my neighborhood, where strange and threatening people might move in down the block, or God forbid next door with parties and blaring loudspeakers. What's mostly invisible to us is that by joining a club we're also saying we're both different from, and probably better than, the people not in the club. All such identities can eventually backfire into religious schism, wars, boundary skirmishes, hurt feelings, and cries of racism, bullying and victimhood. No one wins an identity war; it's always just a schoolyard fight. In terms of sheer numbers of people dead from identity warfare, religion ranks first or second as the instigator of human horror. On a lesser scale, it's even more divisive – separating people from each other – than politics. So why do we hold religious institutions so dear?

Maybe we humans need a place to ask the big questions: What am I, and how am I different from other people and things? What holds it all together? What is my purpose and meaning? We need a physical location where it's safe and sound to ask these questions. They're different from: What is fair? What is mine and what belongs to others? How do I share? Those last ones are social questions whose answers are determined by civil authorities. The problem with religions is that they stray into those civil questions instead of sticking with their own provenance, which is explaining nature as it is. Again: natural law allows; human law limits. Religions often don't differentiate carefully and can substitute human laws – the territory of the superego – for natural law – the territory of an individual's internal quest for meaning.

The *Tao Te Ching* is usually read as two linked but separate works. Simplified, Tao means true nature, while Te means virtue. Natural law and human law. But most religions confuse the two. It's a big problem, and not just in Islam with sharia law. Jesus famously addressed this issue by telling us to render unto Caesar what is Caesar's. What most clerics don't want to point out was that Jesus almost never addressed human law, virtue, or ethics. Politics weren't his job, or he might have been able to save his life. But despite Jesus's lack of discussion about social institutions, there is scarcely a Catholic, Protestant, or Eastern preacher who doesn't talk about social justice from the pulpit. Trying to square ethics with metaphysics is confounding, but every religion does it, and mostly it muddies their waters. In Buddhism, the centerpiece is the eight-fold path, something unknown to Buddha on his own journey to enlightenment. It's a practical, social, and political ethical code at heart. In Christianity, the centerpiece is Paulist morality, the guilt of knowing right but doing wrong. Jesus himself didn't talk about right and wrong, and he found his own way by rejecting the totems and strictures of the religion he was raised in. Buddha and Jesus were two guys with independent minds who noticed things about the very nature of life – or at least how it's interpreted by human beings – that others had overlooked. They shed their superegos and opened up to all the possibilities. Once he had battled with fortune and fame, more or less alone in the desert before he started teaching, Jesus noticed that back in town the losers were having a better time of it than the winners could see. Meanwhile, on a similar personal journey that included adopting and discarding the religions of his culture, Buddha noticed that everything is in flux, decaying and being reborn right in front of our eyes. These were metaphysical inquiries. They were questions of who we are as human beings in a natural and behavioral world that clearly had principles that went beyond biology and ethics.

What demon interferes with these lovely metaphysical systems and drives them toward our superego nags? How does God make its way from an unknowable presence to a stern daddy? How does open-ended philosophical inquiry transform into stifling religious judgments? Maybe in wanting to belong, we open up the superego to force conformity on ourselves. The vile little parasite behind our ears is always in favor of narrow middle-class know-nothing lives.

Remember the lie it told us when we were seven? "If I don't get right with Mommy or Daddy, I'll be thrown out of the family." That becomes, "If I don't get in with the right pack of humans, I'll be thrown to the wolves." Religion can be the pack that relieves me from the fear of being tossed aside. Once my chosen religion has taken that role, any other becomes especially dangerous. And around then, my God becomes the only worthwhile God, and needs to be stabilized and evangelized so that I can help my protective group expand with the single-mindedness of a struggling species in the wild. But for my God to compete, it has to be the *most* omniscient, the *most* omnipresent, and the *most* dominant. As the Jesuit Tom Weston points out: You know you've made God in your own image when He hates the same people you do. It's hard to tell which becomes defensive first, the pack of humans in support of the God, or the God itself. Eventually, though, the superego gets to replicate the bullying defensive posture of both: It's unsafe if you don't conform to your pack's rules, and you're doomed if you don't obey your powerful God.

Atheism can be a metaphysical response to religious conditioning, but eventually it too separates into a defensive position and even its own pack. "I don't believe in God" becomes "I don't trust the opinions of people who believe in God." As a card-carrying atheist much of my life I scorned religious believers. I had my own atheistic superego raging. I promise you that not being superstitious can be as much of an identity as being super-stitious is. Atheism belittled me into conforming to materialist empiricism at all times. Things are things and what you see is what you get; that's all there is. Debate was cut off. No different, really, from cutting off debate at a single view of the afterlife. If I've adopted a standard model of the afterlife and how my ethical choices while alive affect it – maybe a karma model or a Catholic-absolution model or a virgins-awaiting-me model – I've cut myself off from other possibilities. My superego is satisfied so long as I con-form to a single model that can belittle me from changing my opinion willy-nilly. If I'm under the thumb of a belief system – any belief system – I can be molded into a productive cog that evangelizes and builds an ever-expanding support system for my fellow believers. God becomes Daddy or Mommy in exactly the same way that my corporate salary takes care of me and infantilizes me. So, some people replace the fear of the scornful parent with an intermediate scorn of a slightly vengeful God.

But there's a way out; in fact, there are many ways out of God and religion being reduced to a superior parent. I can believe in God without belittlement. But I'm not sure I can know that until my superego has receded.

Plus, the better news is that this happens without my willing it. Simply by getting my defenses out of the way, a more liberated view of God and reality shows up all on its own. For me, it started with the physical lumi-nescence that I described earlier, which emerged as my battles with my parasite wound down. What came next was a series of new attitudes toward people, meaning, and especially the unknown. Whereas I had always assumed that the unknown was unknowable, now it was coming to me left and right in startling concepts and words. One day everything might dissolve into a pervasive unity, and another day each object shim-mered. These experiences would last a moment, or a few minutes, or even an hour. They didn't interfere with my everyday life; they seemed to disrupt only my familiar belief systems. Inadvertently, I had stepped into a path to enlightenment – the kind that the Eastern philosophies and religions discuss – and my interest in pursuing this new universe of meaning and moments quickly intensified. I won't bore you with the details; there are more than enough books describing spiritual metaphysical realms. Most of them sound kind of show-offy. Suffice it that my truth-seeking skills, honed in my youth and pursued as an adult rationalist, were just as relevant to the spiritual enterprise as they had been as a know-it-all in my pursuits of journalism and corporate marketing. The only difference was that like it or not I was pursuing the truth of my own experience, not my culture's or an authority's. And with my parasite out of the way, it was really easy. Without a censor, I was allowed to test out any premise, any set of conditions, and any conceptual galaxy. The same thing happens to my clients, and they get a big kick out of it. Many gods become available, depending on what is arising at the time. There's the God of love, the lover of truth, the Christ consciousness, the non-attached Buddha, the absorption Brahman, the wild animist, the transcendental Emerson, the disruptive Zen Buddha, the self-creative God, the destructive Shiva, the Tao, Allah the revealer, Plato's Good, Aristotle's prime mover, Wicca's four-points warrior, physics' Big Bang, and on and on ... they're all worth visiting. For most of them, I am made up of the same essence as the God at hand is, and so as I visit the conditions of one of these realms, I can't be belittled. I might be humbled, but I'm not insulted.

Another way of putting this is that when my parasite leaves my head, my mind is free to play. Yes, I have my social duties and responsibilities, my concern for the planet and species, but only so much. I'm also allowed to be fascinated by what is, right around me, right now, a new world that beckons and glistens and holds me, for the moment and for my lifetime, there to be noticed, examined, inhaled, and exhaled, with each breath.

How could I not be fascinated by this world after the filters are removed?

SEVENTEEN

LOVE

Mostly I've talked about conflict in its immediate sense. Our defenses suddenly rise, and the craziness begins. Conflict shows up, gets dealt with, and disappears, sometimes in less than a minute. The paradigm is Mom yelling at me for not clearing the table, or Dad criticizing my bat speed. But the superego has more insidious tricks up its sleeve, too. It cloaks us in the continual threat of the constellation of experiences we call "hurt feelings."

It would seem inhuman to live without fear of hurting people's feelings, or fear of having my own feelings hurt. Many people believe that the emotional fabric of feelings gives them their juice and compassion. But what if that's wrong? What if hurt feelings are imposed on us by a parasite that wants us to cower and tremble? What would life without hurt feelings look like?

By the time you were twelve, you didn't recite the "sticks and stones" nursery rhyme so readily. As an adult, don't you believe that other people's words of rejection and insult hurt?

As we noted before, the superego borrowed the words "hurt" and "pain" from the id, probably to add urgency and danger to even the mildest of inconsequential conflicts. But there is no physical entity called a feeling that can be stabbed the way my arm or chest can be. Saying my "feeling" was "hurt" is at most a metaphor. And what exactly is a "feeling?" If I "feel" something literally, I'm using the sense of physical touch, right? The etymology of "feel" traces back to touch (and, oddly, taste). But an emotional feeling can't be touched (or tasted). I can't literally grow an emotional feeling. An emotional feeling can't be amputated. But the metaphor is intact: I say that I've developed a feeling for someone, or that my feelings are cut off. I'm constantly insisting to myself that feelings are real, and don't notice that I'm speaking in metaphor. That's the power of my parasitic superego. Emotional feelings are imparted to me as part of my social training. They are little more than mental habits. My natural state of happiness and acceptance doesn't swing up and down, plummeting into sadness and rising into giddy elation. My natural state is kind of indifferent to the emotions; it's in the middle, hardly disrupted.

You don't have to take my word for it, or the scripture of Buddhist masters who are especially adept at describing equanimity. Just work on your superego for a while and see what happens. For most of my clients, emotional volatility declines markedly. Think of how much your insecurities are reinforced by anxiety – the fear that your superego will punish you for making the wrong choice. Anxiety declines as the superego's grip is loosened, and with it goes the emotional roller-coaster.

"My mom can still seem annoyingly selfish," Adriana said to me during a session. They had been estranged earlier, rooted in her mother's failure to protect Adriana from an abusive father. "But after my work with you, it doesn't get to me so much. The odd thing is that I don't feel as cold to her. When I looked at her from my old vantage point, I pushed her away. Now that I'm not worried that she's endangering me, I can keep her close. I don't even have to forgive her. Hey, her insecurities are her problem, not mine. She's actually quite a kind person in her own way."

Adriana isn't paying so much attention to her mother's surface. She feels warmer even though she is taking her mother's words less seriously. We believe that love and friendship are located in some murky depths of emotions inside us, but they're actually always here and now readily available inside and outside, just blocked by our defenses. In fact, Adriana in her lightness of being is closer to her mother than before. Without words for it, she might even see her mother for her splendid, natural self. Adriana might notice that everybody has a splendid, natural self hidden under their defenses. But first she had to learn about her own splendid, natural self hidden by her personal parasite.

James was downcast, practically defeated, when he first came to me. Growing up in a family of six, he felt unnoticed and misunderstood, but by his mid-thirties he switched to believing that there was something wrong with him. He had a good mid-management job in human resources, and a wife and two kids. But alone, he felt empty and unfulfilled. Maybe he didn't belong on this planet. He wasn't suicidal, just forlorn.

If your default defense is withdrawal, resulting from the worry of not being seen for who you are, then you're in for a lifetime of hurt feelings and self-pity. But the flip side is that you harbor a hidden superpower. Done right, wallowing in self-pity can close the wound. Your advantage is that instead of avoiding or denying the hurt feeling, you actually call it out, which gives you half a chance.

I asked James to try a silly experiment for me. (I don't ask my clients to do things I haven't myself, by the way.) On his lunch break, James would step out onto the San Francisco sidewalks and stroll among the busy passersby, silently repeating in a sing-song voice, "Nobody loves me, nobody cares."

At the next session, James said, "I did what you asked." He laughed. "It was so ridiculous," he said. "It wasn't just that it was childish. It just sounded funny, almost immediately. At first there was this morose feeling, but by the third time I said it, it would lighten up. By the tenth, I was just giddy with it. What's that about?"

Like yours or mine, James's superego has been muttering to him all his life words suspiciously close to: "Nobody loves you, nobody cares." The nasty parasite has almost convinced him that if he doesn't keep shaping up and flying right, he'll be abandoned by all. But when James heard that message out loud in his head, its idiocy and infantile sensibility both came careening home. What had sounded dismal while kept subvocal, once surfaced became ridiculous. Try it yourself. See how many times in public you can recite to yourself "Nobody loves me, nobody cares" before starting to laugh.

Hurt feelings are supposedly caused by insulting words and actions. But the person throwing the insult is just defending their own hurt feelings. Not only are we projections talking to projections, but our hurt feelings are triggered by other people's hurt feelings. This can and does go on endlessly, in loop after loop. Who wins? The superego, which gets me to feel small and hurt and anxious. If I'm belittled, it can have its way with me, control my behaviors, and keep me well within its risk-free routines. I'm small and boring, even to myself. But if I'm not concerned about hurt feelings, its advice becomes trivial to me. I've got other strategies and notions besides its favorites, and as an adult I can choose to act on them.

If you're uncomfortable with the idea that hurt feelings are not a necessary part of your life, you're not alone. Only Buddhist communities seem to embrace this notion wholeheartedly, that negative emotions are unnecessary mental constructions. Most of us believe that humanity is tied to our capacity for grief and that hatred is the opposite of love. I'm not asking you to give up those ideas. But it might be worth it to explore whether you spend more time in hurt feelings than necessary; reducing the burden of hurt feelings is one way to open the door to satisfaction and freedom.

Is it possible to get rid of the capacity to be hurt altogether? I don't know. That's not the point. In my seventh decade I'm triggered by the same things that have always bugged me. But the sooner I can distance myself from the signs of emotional volatility, the sooner I can look at what is going on squarely, without the filter of my superego's urgent demands. Your responsibility isn't to be not triggered; it's to keep your eye fixed on the situation after the initial reaction has passed. The triggered reaction becomes a pesky sideshow, and eventually I can notice that no one's attacking me, I'm not in danger, and I get to make my own decisions. When that happens, I might as well not have hurt feelings. If I do, they pass quickly; they no longer lead to sullen spells, angry outbursts, or sarcastic put-downs. Freedom arrives apace.

EIGHTEEN

BETTER DAYS

We've come to the end. You've heard most of what I know about my superego, its influence on me, and methods to weaken it. The techniques I have shared are the same ones that I used to shift my gremlin out of my head, off my shoulder, and way over there, to the right of me, just outside my peripheral vision. It's far enough away that I can't hear it, and its ugly mug doesn't blemish my view. I have no idea how it spends its days, and I don't care. When it wriggles its way back in, and starts speaking up again, I say, "That's you, my superego." I point an imaginary finger at it, admonishingly. It evaporates like a vampire brought to daylight. It wasn't easy getting to this point in our relationship. It took several years of persistent interest in my own defensiveness. I had to stay with my sufferings – large and small – long enough to become dispassionate and able to abstract lessons. But the rewards along the way were steady and rich. Every time I got my gremlin out of another room, that room opened up to a whole universe of fascinating feelings and objects. My life now is about as ordinary as it ever has been. I have clients, write, garden, cook, watch Scandinavian detective shows in the evening with my wife, and do it all over again the next day. Sometimes I visit friends or family. I lack ambition but get lots of projects done. Meanwhile, I mostly get a kick out of things, find just about everyone fascinating and lovely, and commit to a fraction of the snarkiness that I once engaged. My life feels alive, vulnerable as all get out, and ready for anything or anybody, without fear or favor. And best of all, I'm never short of love.

The cruelest lie told by your superego is that you're unlovable. Every time you feel lonely, or you search for a mate, or start to hate someone, your superego is heartlessly claiming that you don't deserve love. Ultimately, silencing your superego is the same thing as finding love. That might sound enchanting and romantic. It can be, but true love like this is also practical and ordinary. The mechanics are wacky and require some sorting out.

For the superego to enforce its rigid morality – the relentless pursuit of social productivity – it has to make sure you think little of yourself as an individual. You have to care only for your participation in the grind of protecting the species by carrying out social concerns. That might mean doing the dishes for the family, or putting in your eight hours a day. Once you've completed your requirements, your leash can be relaxed a little, but better you use that time to think about tomorrow's tasks than daydream or explore your interior self.

The superego *wants* you to feel empty without social purpose. Your parasite encourages you to feel meaningless, bored and listless, mentally searching for something better than being alone and inactive. That reinforces the notion that *being* a person is worthless unless you're *doing* something. If you're worthless without your productive traits, then you're unlovable at heart. Who would love an empty blob? What value would it have?

And there's the rub. According to the superego, my value is a transaction: Insofar as I'm useful to another, I'm considered worthy and, when appropriate, lovable. As we project our most charming self on others, we encourage them to do the same, and thereby match up in useful loving behaviors. I act like I love you, and maybe you'll act like you love me. As a fairly unique, useful being, I love you, and hope for the same in return. A half century ago, the brilliant psychologist R.D. Laing described this dialogue of one projection to another in his paranoia-inducing book, *Knots*. Here's one of his knots:

> Narcissus fell in love with his image, taking it to
> be another.

> Jack falls in love with Jill's image of Jack, taking
> it to be himself.
> She must not die, because then he would lose himself.
> He is jealous in case anyone else's image is reflected
> in her mirror.

> Jill is a distorting mirror to herself.
> Jill has to distort herself to appear undistorted
> to herself.

> To undistort herself, she finds Jack to distort her
> distorted image in his distorting mirror
> She hopes that his distortion of her distortion may
> undistort her image without her having to distort herself.

Even if you think love between two people is more than a projection feeding a projection, your fear is still that the other person might drift away and leave you. We make all sorts of promises to our loved ones in hopes of preventing abandonment. "I'll be back tomorrow. I'll miss you. Wait for me. I'll be thinking about you today." Why are vows so prominent at a wedding? You'd think that the one time you wouldn't have to worry about loss would be during a rite of attachment. Nope. Marriage vows are public, and society is devoted to the notion that each individual is weak and needs to be restrained, corrected, pushed around, shamed, and kept in line for the purpose of productivity. What a drag.

But if you could shut up the superego and its pursuit of practical use value, you might be lovable, all the time, just by living. Love might not be an episodic occurrence, but a constant state of being, accessible at will at any time.

What if love is just the way things are when I'm not separated from things? Most if not all my separation is defensive, prompted and sustained by my parasite. If I let myself stay connected to other things and people, without distrust, maybe I'll be in a more constant field of love.

Love has different flavors: at any one time it might show up as child-like, romantic, passionate, impersonal, friendly, empathic, forgiving, or compassionate. We think our actions control which kind of love will appear, but maybe that's wrong. I was nearly sixty when I heard some-one say, "Compassion is the love that arises in the presence of suffering." Everything I thought I knew about love disappeared instantly. In that state-ment, no one has control over love. Instead, an already-present field of love bulges and takes the right shape to meet the circumstances. If I'm with a pal, love might be friendly. With a partner, it might be passionate. With the bank clerk, it might be impersonal. I don't choose; the moment does. Can I appreciate love if I'm largely passive in its sway?

Compassion is the form of love that is most common in everyday life. We live among complainers complaining. That makes sense since we've cluttered our civilized lives with so many things and attitudes to acquire, prize, show off, employ, and maintain; any that don't solve our survival needs of food, shelter, clothing, and safety lead us down a rabbit hole of suffering, eventually. Anything acquired is lost, employed is discarded, maintained is broken. Complaining is our artful way of dealing with all that suffering. We complain to rid ourselves of the complaint. We civilized humans complain about just about everything. And at our best, we listen to each other complaining. It's a constant symphony out there. That's all that compassion is: listening as suffering arises. It's us being available to the arising of suffering, and possibly noticing the accompanying field of love that envelops both of us. In the medieval Fisher King tale*, as told by Wolfram of Eschenbach, the grail-seeking knight Parzival finally makes his way to a mysterious martyr in terrible pain who is protecting the holy chalice. The young knight stays respectfully silent, as his mother had taught him to do around elders, and the grail remains concealed. Parzival leaves forlorn. Disgraced for his failure on his quest, the knight spends his next years wandering, jousting, and entertaining life lessons before finding himself back in the martyr's kingdom. On this second visit, though, he speaks the magic words: "What ails you?" The martyr is instantly healed, and the holy grail is revealed and given to Parzival for safekeeping.

"What ails you? Tell me about it." That's all that compassion is: an interest in another person's suffering, devoid of ideas of how to fix it. If we complain to rid ourselves of the complaint, then all we need for healing is someone who will listen. The martyr in the story is Christ, of course, reminding me that empathy requires two attitudes: I'm OK with asking about suffering, and I'm willing to reveal myself as the person asking. It wasn't enough for Parzival to wonder why the martyr was suffering. Like anybody would, he did that on his first visit. We're all curious about suffering. But do we actively engage with another person's suffering, or turn from it quietly in hopes that we won't be reminded of our own?

Compassion is an activity of allowing suffering to expose itself and blossom as if a fascinating rose. And every other form of love operates the same way. Let it expose itself. It's already there, and the only trick is to be interested in what's around you rather than your own so-called needs. If

---

*This version of the Fisher King story was told in the early 13th century by German poet Wolfram von Eschenbach in *Parzival: A Romance of the Middle Ages*, (Mustard/Passage translation, New York: Vintage 1961). Like many a twice-told parable, the ending of Parsifal's acquisition of the Holy Grail has a different moral in other versions. Which reminds me to mention that my Bible interpretations, whether the story of the Garden of Eden or the Sermon on the Mount or any other passing reference, are my own. I tend to steer clear of theologians these days; often they seem to me overly concerned with Caesar's world.

you think you need love, you might never find it.

When your superego quiets, and your defenses recede, first open curiosity, and then love and truth always enter. Curiosity scans your proximity with open joy, and then love appears as you focus on your relational self, truth as you keep a more observational eye. They're fascinating realms, and they combine and separate as your interests change. Fields of love and truth can appear in many ways, and they're in motion always. Lots of books describe these fields, under such labels as nirvana or heaven or self-realization or rapture or enlightenment or whatever. They're all true descriptions – that is, true to the author at the time they had that experience. You might have an experience like one of them, or something completely different. It doesn't matter. Just be prepared for rather spectacular surprises coming to you, your life, and your experiences when you move the defenses to the side. Personally, I try not to predict them or anticipate them; when I do, I've just found another way to suffer. Eventually, when you've dismantled as many defensive postures as you want, love and truth emerge on their own, as in a slacker's dream, arriving without desire or effort. Maybe you were searching for a long time, with your quest hidden inside your repetitive work to remove your defensiveness. Maybe you're Parzival alighting from your horse, skillfully removing your armor, looking around, smiling, breathing the ripe air, and asking, "Hey, what's going on here?"

You might have noticed that I don't talk about getting rid of the superego, annihilating it, or booting it off into oblivion. I'm not certain whether that's possible for a human living among humans. And that's too bad because a little bit of worry can go a long way. But on the other hand, the idea of perfection is its own torture museum. If I don't need to perfect myself, I'm free to putter and bumble around indiscriminately, like a kitten attacking a jerking string or a kid on a zip line traversing a rain forest from above – the kinds of activities that seem a good match for the world of delight. Most of worry and gloom – the habitations of the scornful parasite – feel heavy and black and white. Sometimes old grainy movies are appropriate, though, and the grim world is real, too. Feeling lost can be its own portal to new worlds. Why wouldn't I abide that?

And yet the gloomy, productive, black-and-white, defensive, projecting, preferring, and hierarchical world is a pretty small slice of reality. There are soooo many possible worlds without those lousy conditions. Why wouldn't I want to visit those, and bring them back to my little life as the light and rainbow of possibilities that is here, now, available and shining?

I don't need perfection, and I don't need isolation. If I want to find myself in truth, freedom, love, and contentment – and I think that's a pretty complete list – I need my superego to relax only enough that *most* of life is light, feathery, and fascinating in and of itself. Every time my parasite disappears, I can find my goofy, curious self who enjoys everything around me without needing a thing. Like the song goes, "I got plenty o' nuttin' / An' nuttin's plenty fo' me." When that's true, every day can be full of momentous discoveries, free of my inner critic, truly and lovingly here for the ride.

READING GROUP GUIDE

BETTER DAYS
Tame Your Inner Critic

Talking with Neal Allen

Why didn't I know that my inner critic wasn't me?

Isn't that weird? No one told me that it was a visitor, or a parasite, or a fake mom nagging me. Like everybody else, I thought
I was talking to myself. It wasn't until one day in a therapist's
office where it showed up as a gremlin on my left shoulder that
it occurred to me that it wasn't me. My personal parasite hides
well, and by staying in the shadows – a subvocal whisper – it gets
to pretend all sorts of things: that it's me, that it's smarter than
me, that it's more mature than me, that it's got the best answers.
None of that is true. It's probably helpful for the species for us all
to believe that we're no-good children who need punishment (a
frowning pseudo-parent in this case) to prevent us from causing

damage. For thousands of years, a suspicious and often damning God took care of our belittlement. I think as God's force waned over the last century or two with life-by-science, the superego's ubiquity probably established itself. But actually, most of us don't need a simple-minded scold in order to make the right choice, do the right thing. Our sophisticated, smart, experienced adult self can navigate its own life, thank you very much. By the way, one way to distinguish the real you from your superego is to ask yourself who the parasite has been talking to and scolding all this time.

Why did you write this book?

Some nice people introduced me to my own inner critic/superego. I mention two of them in the book: my late therapist Bob Birnbaum and the spiritual teacher known as A.H. Almaas. Separating from my superego had all sorts of salutary effects. Then when I switched out of my corporate career into executive coaching, I naturally started directing my clients into recognition of their own superegos. It had been a cool experiment for me; maybe they'd find it cool, too. The more I watched them encounter their own little demon, the more I noticed incredible similarities from one person's superego to the next. Those common responses to fixed questions allowed me to trust that I was gaining precise enough knowledge about the practice of identifying and relaxing the superego that I might share it more widely by setting it down on paper. In a way, this book is simply documentation of what I've seen in more than a hundred one-on-one clients, a bunch of workshops, and dozens of more casual dialogues. (At dinner parties, my wife sometimes has me call out a guest's superego as a kind of amusing parlor trick.)

Also, it's my belief that almost all the work toward freedom or enlightenment or heaven on earth is *destructive* – tearing down the defenses that obstruct the beauty around us. Moving the superego to the periphery is the centerpiece of tearing down the defenses. It is the superego, after all, that curates and invokes our defenses against imagined threats. As my superego departed, light entered. It worked that way for me, and that's all I really know in the end. Some of my clients tell me it works the same way for them, so I keep doing what I do.

Your wife, Anne Lamott, writes about her Christian faith. Are you a Christian, too?

Annie likes to say that religion-wise she doesn't have any idea what I am. I'm not sure I do, either. I was raised in a Congregational church that was all about social action, especially what was then the Civil Rights Movement, and not at all about fire and brimstone. For the first four decades of my adult life, I was mostly an atheist. But still I sometimes taught Sunday school, and found that Genesis, Job, and the Jesus parables provided lovely metaphors for living well in the crankiness of civilization. I was in my fifties before discovering spiritual interests, and plowed through Hindu, Sufi, Buddhist, and other esoteric texts before returning to the Gospels, which I found newly engaging and thought-provoking. What do I believe? That Jesus, Buddha, and some others have caught on to methods for breaking through our everyday fears and attachments and hierarchies and landing in an unobstructed field of love and truth. I would say that Annie and I meet up there, too, on some days. But you'll have to ask her.

Is the superego voice always gendered and based on parental figures such as "mom" and "dad"?

There is a deep-seated cultural trope at work here. I'm not in favor of it; I'm just reporting on it. In most modern cultures, the mother figure is the voice who tells the child they are all right inside, and the father figure is the voice who tells the child they are all right in the outside world. Most of my clients, of any gender or sexual identity or upbringing, have a different default strategy for adults who present themselves as women from adults who present themselves as men. It's not all that important, though. In the end, at any one time a superego is just using the tropes to belittle their hosts. Gender stereotypes are the least of the damage, although since most people, men and women, hear the voice as a hectoring woman, the superego has always been one starting place for studying misogyny in our culture.

Sometimes when I look in the mirror, I hear a voice tell me I'm ugly. Is that my superego or something else?

That's your parasite, for sure. It always wants you to start from disappointment. That pushes you into the common social membrane of working to make things better. If you're OK with yourself, you can decide for yourself what to do next. Being satisfied is all there is to sustainable happiness, probably, and your parasite doesn't want that to be revealed. So, what are you going to get out of improving your looks? From making more money than you need? From crushing that third drink? Weirdly, I'm now convinced that no novelty or excitement can trump recognizing my own contentment, and that I can't find more satisfaction than what results from a full belly.

How did you pick your title, *Better Days*?

Music means a lot to me. Back in the day, a guy named Paul Butterfield emerged from the Chicago blues scene with a killer blues band that he based in the Northeast for a number of years. (It was that band that backed up Bob Dylan when he went electric at the Newport Folk Festival.) The blues are mainly about our social problems, our emotional conflicts, the stuff that makes us lower our heads and shake them with a long, sad "not that again." After a while, Butterfield replaced his musicians with a new set and a new sound, which still had the blues, but layered in what was then called jug band music, a lighter, frothier, funkier, more directly optimistic sound. He called that band *Better Days*. Thinking about the book I was writing, that sounded like a movement and a vibe I could offer. Better days, by the way, is well short of any promise that you'll get completely free of the superego. Keeping it at bay is the idea, reducing the number of times a day your superego is influencing your choices.

Most of us have lived under our superego's weight for decades. It has poked its way into all corners of our lives. So it has a big head start, no matter how much we want its habits to disappear. But my most diligent clients, the ones who actively work on it for a few minutes a day, tend to get some freedom in a few months, and those who are disciplined to face off with it for an hour once a week might find a newly peaceful life in a year or two. There are three ways of looking at the point of this work: It's a path to less anxiety. It's a path to more freedom. It's a path to enlightenment. I'd say it's a pretty good path to enlightenment, an excellent path to more freedom, and a pretty sure path to less anxiety. After six months of intent focus on my gremlin, my level of anxiety reduced to a fraction of what it had always been. After two years, I quit believing my story. After four or five years, I came into a consistently available presence. I've seen those kinds of numbers in some of my clients. Like at the gym, it's all in the repetitions.

GROUP ENGAGEMENT IDEAS AND OPENING QUESTIONS

Meet your own superego

Pair up; each pair works alone. Choose who goes first. In the first round, A asks B the series of questions. Once B has reached the end, roles are reversed. B asks A the same series of questions.

1. Where in your physical geography is your inner critic?

2. Pull it out from there and set it an arm's length in front of your eyes

3. What does it look like?

4. What is its expression?

5. Ask it, "When did you take charge?"

6. Ask it, "Who put you in charge?"

7. Ask it, "Why are you still in charge?"

8. Ask it, "I want to take charge for a while. Is that OK?"

9. Ask it, "Are you worried something will happen to me if I take charge?"

10. Ask it, "Are you worried something will happen to *you* if I take charge?"

11. Ask it, "I know this will be hard for you, but I want to take charge for a while. OK? I need a complete affirmation."

12. Tell it, "Great. And I want to thank you for saving my life as a kid."

13. Put it back where it normally lives.

Note: Many people will have a hard time finding their superego the first time. That's OK. If it doesn't show up in two or three attempts, just go through the exercise with the arm outstretched as if you had found it. It will still answer your questions, which is the important thing.

Opening questions for book group discussions

1. How risk-averse is the superego? How conservative? Are its warnings about upsetting the status quo appropriate?

2. If you weren't worried about your conscience punishing you, would you make the same choices?

3. Have you met anyone who seemed to operate without being defensive? What were they like? What might it be like to feel secure in your ability to make good choices?

4. What is the connection between taming the superego and finding peace, God, or freedom?

5. What does the author mean when he says that you don't have to feel guilty for feeling content? How does that square with notions of privilege and unfairness?

FURTHER QUESTIONS

What is the "id" you refer to?

It's a term that Freud's English translators came up with. It encompasses the two biological *instincts* that affect our social behavior, the drive to survive and the libido. The id has its own realm; for instance it might feel predatorial or adrenalized or pleasure-seeking. Its energy tends to be immediate and urgent. Its defenses are the famous fight, flight, or freeze. In contrast, the superego is non-instinctual, relies on cultural norms for its impetus, has to feign immediacy and urgency since it is a mental fabrication, and has its own defensive postures: withdrawal, anger, and superiority.

Can the superego have more than one voice? Can it morph from one voice to another depending on the situation? For example, when I work, I can hear my boss's voice in my head; when I fold laundry, my mother's.

Oh yes. The superego can morph. For a lot of people it can alternate between a snarky bully and an innocent-sounding victim: "Oh, I was just trying to help." Some people actually have a committee of three or four different creatures who apply themselves to different situations. But my guess is that underneath these personae is hiding one master superego. "Master" by the way doesn't imply intelligent. They're all pretty stupid. Bullies don't ever need to be right.

You mention that the superego has developed and starts to take effect by around age seven. What if any effect do the teenage years have on the development of the superego? It would seem that these are impressionable years.

For most people (the exceptions tend to be people who encounter near-death experiences in their teens or later) the lessons received at seven years old are never updated, just repurposed.

Are there more than three defenses? Can a person have a combination of these three defenses? Are there questions I can ask myself to uncover which one I am?

On the instinct side there are fight, flight and freeze. On the social side there are just the three: withdrawal, anger, and superiority. We all have all three. Most of us default consistently to one of the three. Are you the type who withdraws when confronted? Or the type who gets angry? Or the type who acts like a know-it-all? The primary value to knowing is that you can see how consistently you use this one tired defense over and over. It starts to look mechanical, and that tends to lighten it up.

Is self-sabotage a form of defense? How does self-sabotage fit in with the superego?

Usually self-sabotage is the defense of the know-it-all type. The sabotage is a response to the need to be seen as right. As the project or goal comes into focus, the fear is that you won't succeed and so you cut and run. Usually, the problem is that as a know-it-all, you set an idealized goal and not a realistic one. You're determined to be smarter than the average bear, and when the truth that you're just another bear starts to roost, you'd rather not see your impending failure. But if you can conquer the initial idealizing, you can set realistic goals that don't need to be abandoned.

Would positive affirmations help to tame my superego?

I don't do any affirmation work myself. My exercises operate under the assumption that destroying the barriers to light is the sure way in. While I shine light on problems to expose their exaggerations, it's a different kind of light from the clarity that emerges when the problem eventually disappears.

This sounds like social Darwinism or solipsism or Ayn Rand selfishness. How do you combat poverty, climate change, or any other social ill without a superego?

A wild distinction found in most spiritual traditions is that *determinism* – the idea that I'm not in control of things – does not actually lead to *fatalism* – the idea that I shouldn't bother. It turns out that when you're at peace with yourself, and don't have to put on the dog, you're more likely to tap into generosity and kindness in your daily life. Those inborn attributes of kindness, generosity, love, and empathy are less protected and show themselves more easily. Recognizing that you are more the same than different from others naturally leads to amplified compassion and its interest in the comfort of others. You're less *responsible* for others' comfort, and more *interested* in it. And that abiding interest in love for others can develop into lots of different kinds of actions: personal care for others or political activism or charitable contributions or any form of do-gooding. What's more fun than participating in love and what love is more human than compassion?

How do social media and the culture of comparison feed our superegos? Since social media are difficult to avoid, what can we do to prevent this?

Do you ever ask whether you *need* one more friend? What do you gain from another person liking you? What's wrong with some people disliking you? Isn't it easier to live without makeup? Any feeling of insufficiency is curated by the superego. Like advertising, social media amplify our insecurities. The work is always the same: Investigate your beliefs in your own suffering. Whether social media can then be transformed – for you, at least – into a benign way of keeping in contact with people and ideas is a wide-open question.

Is our superego responsible for taking standards and placing those expectations on other people? Or is it just on ourselves?

The superego curates all our hierarchies. As empathic beings at heart, we don't need hierarchies. But the superego doesn't let us have that experience. *All* of my social judgments, the nice ones, and the not-so-nice ones, are being managed by my superego. When I call someone "smart" I'm objectifying them. It might be harmless, but it isn't important to who they are. What's important to who they are might be kindness, availability, inner strength, the sorts of things that while highly abstract are also available to virtually all of us.

Does the superego always creep in at the beginning of things, in the dreaming process, or can it also appear as a sense of dread or self-admonishment after the accomplishment has been earned or when putting it out into the world?

The superego exerts most of its power at the outset of thoughts or projects, limiting our view. But if you engage in a post-mortem ("Ugh, why did I say that to that person?") that's also the superego. Anything that sounds like emotional conflict is engineered by the superego, whether it's conflict with yourself or others.

Will the superego always adapt its internalized ethics to its society's rules and gender norms? When we change the rules of society, does this then free up our superegos individually and collectively?

You're assuming that we can change the rules of society so they're less onerous or somehow better. The rules of society are simply the attempt of the species to reinforce our most biological selves. Being productive is no different from helping others; ethical systems promote helping others of your kind. But you can't have justice and empathy at the same time. They're different worlds. Justice emphasizes right/wrong, good/bad hierarchies. Empathy emphasizes our lovely commonality. Jesus was explicit about this: Render to Caesar what is Caesar's (the world of justice) and God what is God's (the world of grace).

As we get older, do we naturally shed our superegos?

When we're young, we encounter various dangers one by one. Most are social dangers, and they tend to be exaggerated by the superego. As we navigate one problem after another, a little bit of reality sets in. Maybe since I've survived a few clothing catastrophes I might not worry about my clothing so much. While in certain ways people get more rigid as they age, in a lot of ways they get more laissez-faire. Being laissez-faire can be an effective antidote to the superego's mischief.

By "following your nose," does this mean we should let go of to-do lists and accomplishments? And by not attributing value to anything, is this a way to trick the superego into a state of non-self-judgment?

Believe me, your nose will lead you into what other people call accomplishments. We're in a web of circumstances beyond our control that brings us to our current moment. The web includes the species' demands for productivity. It's very hard not to be productive in our current civilization. The main thing that changes when the superego recedes is unexpected; the distinction between work and play blurs. Whatever shows up is just the next puzzle, the next stuff, the next navigation, the next moment. I do a lot of things most days that others would call productive. To me, they're just the next thing that shows up. It works because we never were that much in charge of things in the first place.

Is how we value our time also a reflection of our childhood programming? For example, you say you value time spent tending to the health and welfare of your children, whereas I might value time working towards a career goal.

Valuing time is a fraught condition. It assumes time is a resource that needs to be filled up, and that like a container for money its contents can be wasted, hoarded, spent wisely or unwisely, or filled with worry about impending poverty or doom. But time isn't a resource; it's an abstract notion that we use to measure the passage of events. Clocks are quite helpful in getting packages delivered. Why would I value one circumstance of my life over another? If presence is capable of instant and steady satisfaction, it doesn't need hierarchical value systems. Once my belly is full, anything else I do is secondary. Of course I have responsibilities – the burdens of maintaining the complex circumstances of civilization. But by 11 a.m. I probably have done my share. The rest of my time isn't taken up by concern for civilization. *Even if my activities look productive to others, I don't have any need to create an abstract notion of extra value in order to enjoy my satisfied self.*

Are there instances when the superego is helpful in adult life? For example, if I am abusing substances, does the feeling badly and self-shaming do me a disservice in terms of perpetuating these habits or would it aid in the recovery process to quiet those voices? Or is the superego in this instance in fact trying to "save my life"?

Everybody wants the superego to be a good guy, but it isn't. As an adult, you don't need the voice of an absent parent frowning at you to make your decisions. I can't promise you will make better decisions without a superego, but you'll sure be satisfied more often, and that tends to encourage accommodating ways.

You say that the human being's superego's primal drive is to be productive, but is this true for everyone or can it change as cultural values change?

Does the superego become a friendly ghost? Not really. It's just not smart enough to add much to the sophisticated understanding of the world that just about everyone has by the time they're seventeen. Why would I listen to a seven-year-old? It might be friendly, sure, but it hasn't lived enough to make adult decisions. I'm not arguing against beginner's mind. That's different.

Is the idea of being productive an age-related drive? Not every-one derives value from work, and especially when we are young or teenagers...my teenager doesn't seem to have much drive to be productive, let alone put laundry away. Does this kick in late in life?

Seven hours a day of school and homework on top of it isn't enough productivity? Plus there are hormones at work. The species eventually catches up with just about everyone; there's still a 40-hour work week waiting for you.

Is this generation less interested in productivity and more inter-ested in higher values?

Kids these days! What exactly are higher values? So, they've traded in a fifty-hour yuppie work week for an environmentally conscious career. If the species needs them to work fifty hours a week they'll have to. If the species only needs ten hours a week, great! If the species needs environmentally conscious workers, great! What no one notices is that everyone already is plenty productive. What the superego does is try to convince us *we're not productive enough and things are going to hell in a handbasket*. The scale of what is productive enough changes, but it's always more than necessary. Boomers had to work twice as hard because the population was growing faster than the institutions that were necessary to maintain it. We should feel good that our children and their children have been able to relax the standards. But our kids are saddled with their own discontented ways. It's the same superego whether in my generation it said work more hours or in this generation it says solve the world's problems.

Is impostor syndrome a form of the superego? Why do I always feel I don't measure up?

Impostor syndrome is fascinating. While the superego takes advantage of it, it's also a taste of reality. What is it to think others know more than you and that you're faking it? It's the same thing as investigating your personality. What sits under the personality? Nothing. It's a giant structure that you maintain, reinforce, and expand daily, trying to present the best fake you to the world. Impostor syndrome recognizes that you're mostly reactive, making it up as you go, and trying to present a seamless facade. After suffering impostor syndrome for a while, most people eventually start to notice that everyone else is faking it too, and that underneath it all we'd rather be our goofy lovebug selves than this serious, adult, hard-working picture that works for our boss. A lot of people experience impostor syndrome in their forties, and watch it recede in their fifties. As it recedes, the illusion that there are experts at life also recedes.

It sounds like we form the superego in childhood. Is there anything I can do as a parent to prevent my child from forming these negative voices in their head?

Not a thing! Just notice that no matter how attentive a parent you are, the odds are a gazillion to one that your child will have the same size superego as just about everyone else, and it will torture them in the same way. Yes, I'm offering parents a get out of jail free card. A good enough parent is all that anyone can be. Here's the problem with trying to sidestep the superego's development and domination: Can you tell a child that it is unnecessary to have hurt feelings? Yes, but it's not going to get you anything. It won't make sense to the kid, and it won't stop the child from crying the next time a bully calls them a name. That's just the roughhouse of learning the ropes. It's complicated growing up in a civilization where people are allowed to default to distrust. But that's not a big deal in the end. The superego is damaging mainly to adults, who aren't allowed to mature under its supervision. Just remember to give your kid a superego diploma when they graduate from high school. Tell them: That voice in your head? You don't need it anymore. And suggest that they might want to take up some of this work.

I seem to have a running tape of anticipating what others will think of me and my actions in almost any scenario. Is this my superego? I really would like it to be quiet.

Any time you're projecting yourself into the future in order to protect your emotions you're listening to the superego's rant. One common attitude I've noticed in people who have done this work is that they don't worry about being offended or offending much. They're less likely to be offensive since they're not defending a pronounced self, and it's hard to be offended if you're an open-minded person.

If I was neglected as a child, or had to grow up faster than normal, does this affect the formation of the superego?

Not much that I've seen. If you were beaten severely, that's a different story. But most childhood neglect falls short of survival danger. Growing up faster than normal may push you into the narcissistic posture of needing to be resourceful, and the awful consequence of believing yourself to be superior to others. But if you didn't have that defensive system, you'd have one of the other two, withdrawal or anger, so it's kind of a wash.

I wonder if, in today's society, and especially with social media, does society's influence build the voice of the superego as much (if not more) than parents and caregivers? It seems like social media has more influence on some kids than the family of origin.

The superego isn't a sophisticated machine. It has a few lessons that it repeats over and over. It takes any event in a person's life and feeds it through that shortlist. Life becomes a matter of matching the superego's primitive fairy tales to reality. Social media presents the same kind of fairy tales that parents present that bosses present that religious leaders present that political leaders present. On one side of the fairy tale is the presumption that you are in control of your own life and hard work will be rewarded. On the other side is the reward system of a better standard of living for yourself and others.

Is the root of procrastination the superego?
How do I stop procrastinating?

You're not procrastinating. You're just getting things done in a different order. You get just about everything done, and don't let it go at that. Just about everybody thinks they're procrastinating. Over time, releasing the superego also reduces the amount of emotional capital that otherwise builds up as daunting tasks approach. Somehow the tasks don't seem so daunting, and the possibility of failure is less catastrophic.

Are messages from your superego always negative and harmful? Where do the positive messages I say to myself come from? Is this my superego also or something different?

Most of your thoughts are not the superego. If you engage in a mindfulness meditation practice, you'll notice that most thoughts are fragments, next are simple names of objects, and then a distant third are complete sentences. The superego speaks in complete sentences. But here again, it doesn't necessarily occupy most of your mind space. You have practical thoughts that help you do the dishes, read a book, answer your email, and gossip with friends. There's nothing wrong with your mind; it is relentlessly curious, collecting information about objects near you, hoping to form a puzzle that you can solve. The mind is a playful thing. The superego thoughts are the ones that sound like worry – questioning how you'll be perceived, reminding you for the thirtieth time today what's on your to-do list, rehearsing an imaginary dialogue with a friend or perceived enemy, as well as the thoughts that call you names or otherwise imply that you're not good enough. While they're actually a small percentage of our thoughts, the superego's postures are especially vivid, usually concrete, and tend to return us to disappointment before we've had time to notice our satisfaction with life.

Can our superego be so loud that we put our expectations of ourselves onto others?

Does the superego govern our projections? Sure. The superego objectifies others into ranked orders and finds a way to exaggerate most people's dangers to you. When you look at someone you perceive as an enemy at work, say, you see the enemy so strongly that everything about their face looks insincere. The pathology of malignant narcissists is relevant here. They commonly tip off their own self-doubt by accusing others of the bad behavior they're considering for themselves.

Is the human being's natural adaptation to the rules and constructs of society exactly what will ultimately cause the demise of human beings? Productivity is so ingrained that we burn fossil fuels like there is no tomorrow.

Let's be fair: the human species has been fantastically successful. There are far more human beings on Earth than there should be. If you don't count domesticated animals (cattle, dogs, cats, etc.), the next most populous big lumbering animal might be the kangaroo, with about 15 million individuals. Just feeding and clothing and housing eight billion human beings is an extraordinary achievement; the species would be proud if it had a brain. But the world of Darwinian biology that we live in is mechanical and predictable. Every species rises and falls, and so will human beings. Often a species dies off in a pronounced population collapse. Who knows? The human species has succeeded through adaptations that were mentally produced (antibiotics, food storage, shipping lanes, those sorts of things) but ultimately is always serving the hidden masters of population growth and niche-filling. Those masters are dumb and mechanical, prone to unintended consequences like global warming, and yet they remain the basis for all of our codes of ethics and morals. But ask yourself from your position of one in eight billion, would you rather be worried about the species constantly or reserve a large space for the satisfaction of presence? You'll still be fully productive. You can't help it. You're part of the species. This is *not* promoting social Darwinism; personally, I vote for generous and fair politicians who are sincerely interested in the welfare of others. I just vote with a lightness of being, in the same way that I watch the skyline at dusk.

Does childhood abuse or mental illness affect the size and power of our superego, or make it more difficult to confront and get under control?

I've noticed that people who experienced childhood beatings that verged on the possibility of death take a lot longer to let go of the superego. Presumably, some other people whose true survival has been tested may have more difficulty with this work, too. On the other hand, I have not seen a relationship between the amount of emotional abuse a child received and the size or approachability of their superego. I don't work with schizophrenics, whose superegos can morph into outsized voices that command behavior. As they do with all work that requires self-reflection, malignant narcissists (people diagnosed with a full-on narcissistic personality disorder) have a hard time with this work.

Is there a connection between an out-of-control superego and pain in the body caused by inflammation or an overactive nervous system?

Maybe. I like to point out that there's a quantitative and qualitative difference between what I call the pain of a stab wound and what I call the pain of a hurt feeling. My work doesn't require any belief about emotions translating into cellular activities, so I don't go there.

Can a superego that has not been tamed send us into constant flight or fright?

Superego conflicts aren't susceptible to the autonomic system of fight or flight. In social circumstances, we're not subject to fight or flight. We may want to avoid circumstances, but we either withdraw from them (not in flight but in a sulk) or try to control them with anger (not in a fight usually but in a loud voice) or try to make ourselves seen as smart (through better ideas or snarky put-downs.)

I have never noticed a distinct inner voice. Is there something I can do to be more aware of it?

Ah, your superego is especially clever! (I'm assuming that you feel your life is wanting, or disappointing in some way.) It hides well. First of all, you can probably still pull it out of your head and get into a conversation with it. And the more you act *as if* it's there, the harder it will be for it to hide. How will you know it's there? Simple. If you're in conflict with yourself or someone else, it's there. Period. So, if you notice your hackles rising, point into the air (in your imagination if you're in public!) and say to yourself, "That's you, superego, not me." Over time it will get easier to hear.

Is this work only useful when you find yourself suffering?

Most people I know who've found a spiritual path tell me that it arrived as the consequence of some great heartache, failure, shock, or generalized disappointment in their life. In my early fifties, I was just fine. My career was in full flight, I was getting out of a difficult marriage, my four children were healthy, and I had gathered a lot of interesting experiences in my life. I thought myself about as insecure as the average person, about as satisfied, and probably a little bit more cheerful. My therapist Bob Birnbaum, whom I had hired to optimize my life coming out of the divorce, one day excitedly told me that I should read a passage in a new book. It was about suffering. It seemed quite interesting. Then I sat where I was in the downtown San Francisco bookstore, played afternoon hooky from my corporate job, and read the book all the way through in one sitting. The text was all about how anything I did could be prone to suffering, and probably caused me suffering. I was astonished. I had not known it consciously, but my life was constant suffering, in the Buddhist sense. The book was *A New Earth* by Eckhart Tolle (Vancouver: Namaste Publishing, 1997). Now

I had a big problem on my hands – my own suffering! – and I spent the next decade dealing with it.

Are there other books that are helpful with this work?

Byron Katie has a brilliant method to deal with the superego in real time. Try her seminal *Loving What Is: Four Questions That Can Change Your Life* (New York: Harmony 2003, Revised 2021). Eckhart Tolle's *A New Earth*, of course. I no longer differentiate much between inner critic work and general spirituality, so this work can be amplified by traditional works such as the *Tao Te Ching*, *Bhagavad Gita*, poetry of Rumi and T.S. Eliot, and the Diamond Heart series by A.H. Almaas.

Acknowledgments

I am most grateful to my clients for trusting that I'm not a random sadist as I torture them week after week, forcing them into their suffering so it can maybe depart. Our sessions are often filled with an appreciation of pure love, and that feels good. No one of my clients is a lab rat, and nor am I, but like everything else in life, this is an evolving experiment, one that they and I have undertaken unwittingly. The exercises and tools in the book all were developed jointly by my clients and me over the past few years and hours and hours of practice.

In terms of producing the book and getting it out to you, my deepest thanks go to my brilliant agent, Sarah Chalfant of the Wylie Agency, who found the perfect home for it in Namaste Publishing, and to Mary Kellough who presides over that house with the greatest care, gentleness, and precision. For me the hardest part of writing is publishing, and you two make it far more joyful than it should be.

Meg Lundstrom first offered me good writerly advice more than thirty years ago, and I keep going back to her for more. Thank you Meg, and newcomer David Allen, for picking at my blind spots, protecting me from myself, and helping amplify what works. Kent Allen saved me much embarassment. Good readers are hard to get, and I'm lucky to have the three of you.

And finally, as I said once before, there's Annie at my side with her pen and heart, both of which are more refined than any other I know. If everybody had an Annie, the world would be a much better and more loving place, and lots funnier.

Author Photo by Sam Lamott

NEAL ALLEN is a writer, spiritual coach, and speaker whose chief interest is removing obstacles of the ego. A former journalist and corporate executive, he holds a master's degree in Political Science from Columbia University and one in Eastern Classics from St. John's College. He lives with his wife, the writer Anne Lamott, in Northern California.